More Than Chocolate:

Lenten Sermons that Matter

To Beth with blessings for the journey.
Love, Julie

Julie Schaaf

Parson's Porch Books
www.parsonsporchbooks.com

More Than Chocolate: Lenten Sermons that Matter

ISBN: Softcover 978-1-951472-23-8

This book is dedicated

to my husband Danny

and my children Katie and Carter,

with thanks for their constant love, support and encouragement.

Acknowledgements

Thanks to my dear friends Allyson Helvie, Debbie Foster, Susan Williams, Molly Fitzpatrick, Billie Sims, and Margie Dobbins who encouraged me to pursue this. They always have my back! Special thanks to Kitty Olson who hounded me to death until I agreed to take on this project. Kitty also did some proofreading, brainstorming, gave me a marketing plan and has in general been my right hand on this project. Thanks to my cohorts in crime at work Debby Keaton and DJ Wall for living with me while I write sermons. And much love to the disciples at Nazareth Presbyterian Church in Moore, SC, who listen to me each week and love and encourage me in every way possible. Being your pastor is one of my greatest joys.

Contents

The 'I Am' Statement of Jesus

Sermons Matter

Parson's Porch Books is delighted to present to you this series called Sermons Matter.

We believe that many of the best writers are pastors who take the role of preacher seriously. Week in, and week out, they exegete scripture, research material, write and deliver sermons in the context of the life of their particular congregation in their given community.

We further believe that sermons are extensions of Holy Scripture which need to be published beyond the manuscripts which are written for delivery each Sunday. Books serve as a vehicle for the sermon to continue to proclaim the Good News of the Morning to a broader audience.

Rev. Julie Schaaf provides her readers and hearers with good examples of sermons that are thoughtful, practical, and spiritual. We are proud that she is part of this series.

We celebrate the wonderful occasion of the preaching event in Christian worship when the Pastor speaks, the People listen and the Work of the Church proceeds.

Take, Read, and Heed.

David Russell Tullock, M.Div., D.Min.
Publisher
Parson's Porch Books

Words from the Cross

A Word from the Cross: Forgive

Isaiah 43:19-19(a), 25; Luke 23:34

One of the best books I have ever read is actually a children's book entitled Because of Winn Dixie by Kate DiCamillo. It is about a little girl named India Opal Buloni who moves with her father, The Preacher, to the small, fictional town of Naomi, Florida. Opal's mother ran off when she was a baby, leaving a huge hole in her life. The book begins as she goes off to the grocery store to get a tomato for her father and comes home with a big, ugly dog whom she names Winn-Dixie.

Throughout the book, Opal collects a group of misfits as her unlikely friends to fill the space left by her missing mother. One is Otis, who runs the pet store where Opal helps out to pay for the leash and collar that Winn Dixie proudly wears. Another is the local librarian, Miss Franny Brock. Then there is Gloria Dump who is nearly blind but sees with her heart. Opal checks out books from Miss Franny and then reads them to Gloria.

One day, Opal tells Gloria that has learned that Otis spent some time in prison and wonders if she should be afraid of him. It is at this time that the wise, old Gloria Dump, leads Opal to the back of her yard to see the huge tree that has bottles hanging from every branch. Gloria tells her that the bottles keep away the ghosts of all the things she has done wrong in her life. Opal is astounded as she tells Gloria that she cannot imagine that she has done THAT MANY bad things, as she is the nicest person Opal has ever met.

In response, Gloria passes on some wise words and some of the best theology that I have ever heard. She says, with regards to people and their pasts, "You can't judge people by what they done. You got to judge them by what they're doing now!" Whether she understood it or not, Gloria had a real handle on the meaning of Lent and Ash Wednesday.

But even more than that, Gloria's words are reminiscent of the words that the Lord gave to his people through the prophet Isaiah. The children of Israel had been taken into Babylon as punishment for their sins. They had not lived as covenant people. They had worshiped other gods and not demonstrated the love of Yahweh, the God of their forefathers, to the people that they encountered. They had done nothing to be a light to the Gentiles, as God had charged them to do.

The consequences of their actions had landed them as reluctant visitors in Babylon, where they would remain as a people for 70 years. While they were treated fairly, and even allowed to hold jobs and buy property, the sacred center that held their world together had been destroyed. The Temple in Jerusalem was no more. So while they had a certain amount of freedom, they had no political or religious power.

In fact, it was at this time that the feelings of chaos in their lives led an unknown Israelite to pen the words of this Psalm. "By the rivers of Babylon – there we sat down and there we wept when we remembered Zion. How could we sing the Lord's song in a foreign land?" (Psalm 137:1) Do you hear the sadness, the melancholy, the utter despair in their cries? Of course, you do. Because at one time or another, we have all wondered if God has given up on us? We have all thought to ourselves: there is no way God can forgive something we have said or done. We have all cringed with regret at the sins of our omissions. We have all struggled with forgiving someone else. Yet, God sent these words to them and us to remind us that God does not look back and neither should we.

"Do not remember the former things or consider the things of old" came the reply of the Lord to his children living in Exile. Or in other words, I am not going to judge you for the things you've done! I will only judge you for what you are doing now!

But the Israelites, being mere mortals, did just that. They looked back at what could not be changed. They lamented over their past sins, their inability to follow the commandments that Moses gave them in which he said very plainly would lead to blessings and life. They grieved the negative influence that others had on them or the people who had acted unjustly towards those they loved. Just like we look back on the mistakes we made last year and last Sunday and yesterday and this morning! We lament to ourselves with those two useless words – "IF ONLY."

If only she had been kinder . . . if only I had not judged so harshly . . . if only he had told me the truth . . . if only the doctor had looked more carefully at the MRI . . . if only he hadn't been driving after dark . . . and on and on, we, too, judge the things that others and we have done.

Jesus left a powerful example for us with regards to our past mistakes as he hung, dying on the cross. In a word: forgive. He did not even judge the people who gathered around to watch the spectacle that was being made of his life. And he had so much more to judge than we do. You see the people who feared Jesus, the people who did not take the time to understand his radical call to love and his examples of inclusiveness and forgiveness arrested him for blasphemy and treason.

And his own followers were so afraid of what might happen to them if they spoke the truth about who he was and about the miracles that they had witnessed, stood by silently and watched him receive punishment for a crime he did not commit.

But Jesus understood their weakness as he understands ours too. And so as he hung on the cross, dying for you and me, he offered this word about all of us. "Father, forgive them, for they do not know what they are doing." (Luke 23:34) And in saying this, he echoed the words that the Heavenly Father had sent through Isaiah when he said to the Exiles, "I, I AM HE, WHO BLOTS OUT YOUR TRANSGRESSIONS AND I WILL NOT REMEMBER YOUR SINS." Jesus said I am not judging you for the things you done, I will only judge you for the things you do now!

So friends, Ash Wednesday is our time to hold on to these wonderful promises. Promises given to a people in despair and promises made by our savior at the time of his death. Ash Wednesday is a time to examine our lives very honestly and closely and to understand how we can make today better instead of wasting time lamenting over what happened yesterday.

One of the devotions I read last week said, "If we have one foot in the regrets of yesterday and one foot in the worries of tomorrow, we have nothing left to stand on today." Jesus wants us to stand in today and believe the Gospel of forgiveness.

But please understand one important thing. Ash Wednesday is not just about forgiveness, it is also about repentance – about doing better. And while we are not called to dwell on the past, we must recognize our sinfulness in order to make today better. So Ash Wednesday and Lent and repentance are not just about simply going around and saying you are sorry. True repentance calls us to a new way of life.

I like the way that Frederick Buechner explains it, "To repent is to come to your senses," he says. Then he adds, "It is not so much something you do as something that happens. True repentance spends less time looking at the past and saying, 'I'm sorry' and more time looking to the future and saying, 'WOW'!"

I think what Buechner means is that repentance involves change. It does not mean boasting about how you were able to say I am sorry but realizing that if you completely change the way you think and act with regard to an area of sinfulness in your life, you can say "WOW. Look what God has done with me now!"

It is my prayer that tonight's service will be more than symbolic for everyone here. I hope that we will do more than write something on the pieces of paper we've been given, drop them in the basket and feel forgiven. Because the ashes are not just a symbol of our worship but a reminder of the hope that Jesus offers in this word from the cross. It is my prayer that whatever area of your life that you have chosen to reflect on during Lent, that you will remember that Jesus' word is not a word of judgment but a word of encouragement.

As you come forward for the imposition of ashes, Dave and I will say to you, "Repent and believe the Gospel!" Repent is what Jesus calls us to do every day when we claim to be his disciples. And the Gospel, the good news, is that forgiveness is free to everyone who believes in him. And the word from the cross is that, once we have repented, Jesus does not judge you for the things you've done – only for what you choose to do now. Amen.

A Word from the Cross: Community

Psalm 116:1, 2, 12-14; John 19:25-27

As we begin the Lenten journey with Jesus and turn our hearts and minds towards Jerusalem, through the Garden of Gethsemane to the courtroom of Pontius Pilate and finally to the cross of Calvary, the writers of the Bible give us a beautiful insight into the very soul of the Messiah. Authors and composers over the years have referred to these glimpses of Christ's heart as the "Seven Last Words on the Cross", although in truth, Jesus says more than seven words.

During Lent, I will offer an interpretation of each of these words that Jesus gives us and, with the Spirit's help, invite us to reflect on what they mean to us today as modern-day disciples. During our Ash Wed. service, we heard the first word: FORGIVE.

Of the gifts of words offered by Christ on the cross, the word that we heard this morning has always puzzled me the most. "Woman, here is your Son! Here is your mother!" As we listen to each of these thoughts during the Lenten season, you will see that all of Christ's other words were either words of comfort to us or words spoken to fulfill the Scriptures. But this word, at least at first glance, seems more like an affront. As if Jesus is saying, "Mary, look at the child you are losing." And as a mother and grandmother myself, this word seemed just too harsh.

Even the second part, "Son, behold thy mother", as King James records it, could be interpreted as another burden that

Jesus is adding to the beloved disciple's plate after his death. But the Spirit urged me to look past my negative impressions and when I did, I realized that this word is Jesus' effort to create a family, a community, before his death.

In Jesus' day, one's family of origin determined your whole life, your complete identity, and your entire future. By this I do not mean that family is about that nosy question that we often ask here in the south, "Sugah, what does YOUR daddy do?" No, in Jesus' day you didn't have to ask this question. If your daddy was a fig farmer, YOU were a fig farmer. If your daddy was a Pharisee, YOU were a Pharisee. If your daddy was a fisherman from Galilee, you MARRIED a fisherman from Galilee. And what your daddy did determined, for life, your social, economic, and even religious status. Your family was who YOU were. But I believe that, on the cross that day, Jesus formed a new kind of family. A new kind of community, ultimately called the church.

In the community that we call church, we are thrust together with people of different backgrounds, races, social status, needs and sometimes even beliefs and told that, because we are family, we must stick together. I believe that Jesus initiated this idea on the cross when he gave his mother to his beloved disciple. And as it turns out, it was a wonderful idea!

Because when you think about it, the diversity of the group that gathered at the cross sounds more like the people in our day. In our community. People who have different needs and backgrounds who find themselves woven together by some common thread. Think about those gathered at the foot of the cross that day. Some gathered out of morbid curiosity, some out of a need to shout, "Crucify Him", some out of sadness to weep as their loved one suffered, some out of fear as to what would become of them. What I mean is that they were there for a variety of reasons, but at the end of the day, they all had one thing in common – THE CROSS.

And because we are a community of faith, we have the same thing in common. We are a community of the cross. And in today's divisive times, where people almost seem to be looking for things to argue about, we need this vivid reminder. So what does it mean for us to belong to the Community of the Cross?

First, this word from Jesus reminds us that the cross itself joins us to Jesus in his baptism and therefore, in his resurrection. In baptism, we are adopted into a larger family – the church family – that will help nurture us in the Scriptures and their meaning for our lives. And ultimately, it is our baptism that calls us into service in the church family that we have been joined to.

The story is told of a two-year-old child that was being baptized one Sunday. The minister leaned the child back over the holy font, dipped his hand into the water and dribbled it on the toddler's head. Evidently, not pleased with his newly wet status, the young boy pulled himself up, leaned directly into the minister's lapel mic and declared: "You are a bad man!"

Of course, this newest member of God's family did not understand the symbolism of being cleansed of his sins. But as we get older, we realize that being a disciple in the community of the cross calls us to a different standard of living than people of other communities who do not have Jesus Christ as their head.

I believe another reason that Jesus offered this word in the midst of his suffering was to make a statement to those who had put him ON the cross. You see, while the principalities and powers of the day believed that they were tearing Jesus' family apart by taking him away from his followers, Jesus is busy putting it back together.

So this word is a statement of assurance that, as members of the community of the cross, we do not have to be alone unless we choose to. That we have given brothers and sisters in Christ to help us. Family who will laugh when we laugh, rejoice when we rejoice and weep when we weep. Indeed, my celebrations are yours and your sorrows are mine as we walk the way of Christ together.

That is why it seems easier in a church to reach out to someone who has lost a loved one, even if you don't know them well. Because you know that they have the hope of resurrection undergirding their sorrow. That is why we offer to Mentor confirmands and volunteer to teach Bible School and pay $160 for Frances Lynch's pound cake at the Youth Bake Auction. Because the church – your community of faith – was directed by Jesus on the cross to stand with one another in all times and in all circumstances. And in many ways, for those who don't have family nearby – because of death, distance or disagreement – the church can and will be their family.

And amid the tumult of suffering on that night so long ago, I wonder if Jesus recalled the refreshingly simple prayer offered in the Psalm that we just heard. The "pray-er" of the Psalm promises lifelong devotion to God because his prayers for help have been answered. And I know that personally, many of MY prayers for help have been answered when God sent someone ***in this church*** to encourage me, uplift me, admonish me, or comfort me at just the time when I needed it most. Perhaps, as Christ committed Mary and John to each other's care, he was setting the stage for them and for us to be reminded of our blessings when we care for one another in the community that we call our church home.

And lastly, we might consider that by giving his mother into John's care, Jesus set the role model that the church community has followed. Not only are we to care for our parents, our children, those we promise to nurture at their baptism and that we mentor through Confirmation. As the community of faith established on the cross, we are called to care for the greater community – all of God's children.

We do this when we take the time as we hurry through the grocery store to pick up extra applesauce to go into a child's backpack that might be hungry all weekend without it. We do this when we set aside four hours to go to the Soup Kitchen and not only feed the hungry but nourish their souls with hope and a smile. We do this when we put our change in an envelope every night when we empty our pockets to give on the last Sunday of the month during Pennies for Hunger. There are so many ways that we, the beloved disciples of Jesus' community today, have the opportunity to take the tired, the lonely, the hungry, the lost into our hearts, arms and prayers.

And after all, Jesus once said in his earthly ministry, "Whoever does the will of God is my brother and sister and mother". (Mark 3:35) By giving Mary and John to each other at his death, he is reminding us of the creative ways that the will of God may present itself in our lives.

So while this word may at first seem harsh, after examining it more closely, I have decided that this word was indeed a tender word of love to his mother and his friend. He offered them out of his humanity, the suffering he was feeling at knowing how his death would affect them so. AND he offered them out of his Divinity, which enabled him to consider their needs in the midst of his own personal misery.

James Montgomery Boice says that in his words to John and Mary, Jesus created a new society. This society is not segregated according to race or nationality. It is not predicated upon social standing or economic power. It consists only of those whose faith meets at the cross and whose expectations of forgiveness flow from it as well.

As we come to the table of our community – that is the meal that Jesus shared with his disciples before he went to the cross, we see again the beautiful blending of human and divine that makes Jesus' new community so unique.

We eat ordinary bread and drink ordinary juice and remember the EXTRAORDINARY love and grace of God. We remember that the great legacy that Jesus gave us on the cross was the forgiveness of our sins *and* the legacy of his victory over your death and mine. And the bread and the cup remind us all of the new community that Christ gave us on the day of his death. A community of faith and hope where all are welcome. In the name of the Father and of the Son and of the Holy Spirit. Amen.

A Word from the Cross: Trust

Romans 14:7-9; Luke 23:44-46

When I was serving as Chaplain at the Presbyterian Community, I learned that very few Christians are afraid of death. If you have given your heart to God, then death means Eternal life and, while none of us really knows what Heaven is like, we are assured that it is a glorious place. Free from pain, illness, conflict and doubts. Our Scriptures tell us this often. And this is what allows us, as people of the Risen Christ, to be hopeful as we celebrate the resurrection of someone we love.

But I ***have*** learned in my ministry that many people, even Christians, ***ARE*** afraid of dying. Of how they are going to ***get*** to Heaven. That's why Kenny Chesney sings, "Everybody wants to go to Heaven, but nobody wants to go now." But this rings true because we are afraid of the process, not the destination. Let's be honest – everyone's real hope is that one day, you will just wake up dead.

Jesus, our Lord and Savior, had three long hours to die. Three hours of extreme pain and torture and suffering on our behalf. I wonder what any one of us would do in this situation. Well, our God made flesh spent those hours talking to his Father and talking to those around him. And in doing so, he not only left us beautiful words of wisdom, love and promise of hope. He also gave us an example of how to live.

As I have studied the "Seven Words from the Cross" as they are known, I have prayed for the Spirit to give me ONE word each week to share with you and this week, the word I heard was TRUST. "Father into your hands, I commend my Spirit." Many of us would wonder why Jesus felt it necessary to utter this, knowing that he would soon return to Heaven from whence he came. Perhaps Jesus was offering this word for US, so that we could learn what it really means to trust our Lord. Here is what I believe Jesus was telling us.

In Greek, the word "commend" or "commit", as some translations read, means to trust for protection. Jesus is saying that he is willing to give God everything he has – his work, his struggles, his joys, his pain, his family and yes, even his death, because he knows that, when all is said and done, God will protect him. God will be with him until the end. God will make the suffering have a purpose. And I believe that Jesus is reminding us not only that we can die with God, trusting in God's mercy but that we can fully live for God, trusting in God's grace. This sounds poetic, almost romantic. But here is what it really means.

It means that we cannot go to church on Sunday and speak kindly to one another and praise the choir and show appreciation to our Sunday School teacher for a lesson well taught and then go home and yell at our spouse and kids. It means we can't go to Youth Group and listen respectfully and pray with our "church" friends and then go to school tomorrow and ridicule the way someone wears her hair or be disrespectful to our teachers. It means that we cannot go to Circle or Fellowship Club and read the Scriptures and pray with one another and then go out in the parking lot and gossip. Giving your life to God means giving ALL of your life. Not just when it I easy. Not just when it is convenient.

Giving your life to God means loving people who are unlovable and forgiving people who do unforgiveable things. It means doing what is right rather than what is popular. No, we cannot commend our lives into God's hands on Sundays and then take them back the rest of the week. And this is not always easy. Because life is hard and people are not always, well, pleasant. And reality tells us that trusting your life into God's hands does not mean living without pain.

I really think there are people who try to hold onto the myth that, once you become a follower of Christ, life will be all beauty and joy. But anyone with a lick of sense knows that this is not the case. I would love to stand here and say that if you are a Christian that you will never suffer but I try never to be dishonest, especially in the pulpit. The truth is that if a Christian hits his thumb with a hammer, it will hurt just as badly as if he were a Buddhist or an Atheist. And followers of Christ die of cancer and are abused and grow tired and hungry every day. But God does promise us that God will never allow anything worse to happen to us than happened to his Son. And where does that leave us?

It leaves us putting our most valuable possession – OUR LIVES, not just our deaths – into the hands of God. But when you think about it, this really should not be hard. God gave each of us life to begin with. So it is only right that we will give it back to him. However, the truth is that when you give your life to God, it can be pretty scary because you never know what God will do with it! Jesus' prayer on the cross, as he faces the worst circumstances that anyone could imagine is this: I trust you God to use even this for your glory.

I recently shared the very long story about my call to ministry with our youth. I happened to be at Montreat, attending a conference for Christian Educators because I ***thought*** that is what God wanted me to do. My husband was very excited since I volunteered so much at our home church. He saw this as a way for me to get paid for doing what I was already doing.

However, while I was there, the Lord made it clear to me that God's plan for my life was to become an Ordained minister. Our children were 5 and 9 years old. I had no idea what qualifications I needed to have in order to pursue this. But I knew without a doubt that it was God's plan. When I came home and told my husband THIS newsflash, after the initial shock, he agreed to educate a THIRD child, namely me, and began paying tuition to Erskine Seminary.

I did not return to Montreat for 7 more years and, on the morning, I was to accompany a group of residents up to see the new chapel there. Danny admitted that he was pretty nervous about me going. When I asked him why he said, "Last time you went to Montreat, it ended up costing me a bunch of money." My response was, "Oh, you don't need to worry. The only place left for God to call me is to the mission field and even GOD wouldn't ask me to go somewhere if I couldn't take my electric rollers!" But friends, it doesn't really work that way. When we give our lives to God, we truly are offering to have God do with that life as God wills.

I also believe that in this word on the cross, Jesus was teaching us how to pray. Jesus was letting us know that when we are facing darkness, depression, addiction, grief, fear of the unknown, or the valley of the shadow of death, we can trust

God to face life's challenges with us. We can ask God to walk with us through the valley, to laugh with us in our joys, to hold us when we weep, and God will do just that. Methodist minister Will Willimon says that when we take the life that God has graciously given us and give it back to God, it is the greatest act of stewardship. I believe the best way to convey this to our Heavenly Maker is through prayer. In this way, we are sincerely seeking God's will and trusting God to use our accomplishments and our failures for our good and God's glory.

And I will tell you honestly, that this has always been my favorite word from the cross because, according to tradition, this word is a word from Jesus' own childhood. You see, historians tell us that, just as we teach our children their first prayers at bedtime, "Now I lay me down to sleep", Hebrew women taught their children to pray, "Father, into your hands I commend my spirit." Isn't that beautiful?

Even as Jesus hung, broken and bleeding, dying on a tree, he remembered the assuring words that his mother taught him to offer God as he went to sleep each night. So not only was he remembering his Father, but in a way, he was remembering his mother too. What joy it must have brought to her heart, as she stood close enough to the cross for him to see that she would never leave him. Jesus trusted God in death with all that he had because his mother had taught him that this is the best way to live. Trusting God with each day.

This prayer is what brought to my mind the verse from Romans that we heard earlier, one that is often read at Memorial Services. "We do not live to ourselves, and we do not die to ourselves. If we live, we live to the Lord, and if we die, we die to the Lord; so then, whether we live or whether we die, we are the Lord's."

And Jesus' complete trust in God, even in his suffering, along with Paul's instructions to the church of Rome kept one question burning in my mind. So I will pass that question on to each of you for your consideration. That question is WHY WAIT? Why wait until we are dying to trust God with our lives at the end. Jesus didn't.

Jesus left the comfort of his earthly father's carpentry shop to live a nomadic life of poverty and constant struggle because he knew it was the will of God. Jesus confronted the Pharisees and other religious leaders of the day because he knew God sent him to preach that love is more important than legalism. Jesus prayed in the Garden, "not my will, but yours."

And in the end, he trusted God with his life and his death. Years ago, when I first learned that Jesus' mother had taught him this prayer, I decided to make it my own. Personally, I find if I pray too long at night, I usually end up falling asleep because I am too tired to tell God about my day, which God already knows about any way. So I end each night by simply praying, "Into your hands I commend my Spirit."

But if I am going to try to live the lesson of trust that Jesus offered on the cross, why wait until nighttime? So I have decided to start each day the same way. Commending my spirit into God's hands before I get up AND as I lie down.

Jesus thought it was important enough while he was dying on the cross to remind us to trust in the Lord always. If it was that important to Jesus, then perhaps it should be that important to us as well. Amen.

A Word from the Cross: Understanding

Psalm 22:1,2,19-24; Mark 15:25-41

I am going to ask you to open your minds and unclutter your hearts and lend me your imaginations for a few moments if you will.

My name is Cornelia. I am the wife of a Roman Centurion here in Jerusalem. But until a few months ago, we were living near the Sea of Galilee in the garrison town of Capernaum. My husband had a wonderful encounter there with a man named Jesus of Nazareth, which is why we were sent here. I am sure the Governor of Rome meant to punish him for his unfaithfulness to the king by sending us here to the city of David, the Jewish king of long ago. But because of that punishment, I too have had my own encounter with this rebellious rabbi. But I'm getting ahead of myself.

I was pleased when my parents informed me that they had arranged a marriage with Marcus, a man of respect in our village and one very pleasing to my eye. Although he was a soldier, he was different in many ways. He did not have a cruel streak – a need to inflict pain on others, as some soldiers do. He DID have an authoritative presence and has always been a good judge of character. A good decision maker. So I was not surprised when they elevated him quickly to Centurion, commander over 80 – 100 men on any given day.

This has been wonderful for Marcus, who was able simply to command the armies without having to do so much of the real killing. Truth be told, he did not have the stomach, or the heart, for such violence. He often told me that he was glad that the soldiers were able to beat and torture their prisoners because many of them had so much anger. He hoped they got their aggression out on the criminals in their charge and therefore had none left to take home to their families. AND, it has also been wonderful for me because his status enabled us to have servants in our home, to help me with the cooking, cleaning, gardening and marketing so I could pay attention to our four children.

But because he has such a sympathetic disposition, my husband soon began to treat our household help more like family. Which did not surprise me at all. He really is a loving man. And when our gardener fell ill, Marcus did a very brave thing. You see, it was about the time that stories were being told all over Israel about this man named Jesus. Stories about miraculous healings and bold acts of defiance to the religious leaders of his people. He seemed to have quite a following and also quite a mind of his own. Some Jews even claimed he was their long-awaited Messiah.

When our servant became suddenly paralyzed with no apparent cause it just broke my husband's heart. He was really only a boy – barely fifteen – and I know Marcus was thinking of our own son, just a few years younger, and how saddened we would be if we were facing such a hopeless situation. So when we heard that this Jesus was coming through Capernaum, Marcus dared to approach him and ask him to cure the lad.

As soon as he spoke, Marcus felt he had done wrong. As Romans, we are to bow only to the Emperor, so he knew he had not only been unfaithful, but that he was probably wasting his time. If this man were really the Messiah of the Jews, surely, he would not help those who were not his own. But even as he spoke, he felt a connection. And Jesus said to him, "Shall I come and heal him?"

My husband was shocked and replied with humility, "Lord, I do not deserve to have you come under my roof. But just say the word, and my servant will be healed." Yet, when Jesus heard this, Marcus said he was amazed and said to everyone there, "Truly I tell you, I have not found anyone in Israel with such great faith." And before Marcus came home to see it with his own eyes, the boy got up and began to leap around.

Well, news spread to the authorities about what my husband and done. One day his superior called him in and said, "If you have so much faith in this Jesus, let's send you to that hotbed, Jerusalem, so you can see firsthand that he won't be able to get out of the mess he is in now." This was a few months before those who were afraid of Jesus managed to have him arrested and charged with blasphemy and treason. As I said, it was a way to punish my husband. Jerusalem has become a very dangerous place. And uprooting our family from where we have always lived, out of our home, into strange surroundings was hard on all of us. But it is because of this move that I found myself at the foot of the very cross where Jesus was crucified.

It was the most terrible thing I have ever seen. Yet, I had such a fascination with Jesus that I could not tear my eyes away, even from the torture he received. After his arrest and trial, he was held overnight in a dungeon and then brought before the people who called out furiously, "Crucify him! Crucify him!" I couldn't believe how quickly the mob mentality spread to people who didn't know Jesus at all. It is amazing how fear and ignorance can so easily lead to rage and hate.

Then they stripped him and flogged him and put a crown of thorns on his head to mock the claim that he was a king. And he struggled from pain and humiliation as he pulled that heavy cross up the hill to the place they call The Skull where he was crucified him between two common criminals.

But in the midst of all this pain and horror, I noticed a group of women who seemed to have a genuine love for him and so I sort of attached myself to the back of their group and followed behind. I just had to see for myself if this man who had saved our servant, while never even being near him, would save himself. I felt sure that he would.

As I listened to the women around me, it became apparent that they had been members of his inner circle for several years, had been a real part of his ministry. Something I could not imagine. No wonder this Jesus was in so much trouble. Women after all! Such a rule breaker. And yet he seemed so calm, so in control. I am fairly certain by her words that his own mother stood just in front of me because at one time, he said, "Mother, behold your Son" and looked right at her. I couldn't hear the rest of it because the mob around us was so loud, but whatever he said seemed to reassure her at the time.

By the sun and by the aching in my legs, I think we had been there about three hours when, almost as if on cue, the crowd quieted for a moment and Jesus cried out loudly, "My God! My God, why have you forsaken me?" This was all it took for his enemies to begin to mock and deride him even more. Taunting him with things like, "If you really are a king, why don't you save yourself?" And many of the women around me began to sob even more violently.

But I will tell you, there was such dignity and majesty in his cry. Oh sure, it was pathetic. After all, he was 33 years old. He had been mistreated and maligned, humiliated publicly and physically tortured for hours. Who wouldn't cry out to whatever God that came to his mind? But Jesus' cry was more of a personal disappointment. And at that moment, I understood that he was talking to a God who really knew and cared about his people.

I can't imagine. As I said before, we are to claim only the Emperor as our God and the truth is that he doesn't give one whit about our lives. If he had walked through the mob right then, as a citizen of Rome, I would be expected to bow down to him. But I certainly didn't call on him for help when my twelve-year-old sister fell from a boat into the Sea of Galilee during a storm and drowned. As I wept for the emptiness of the palate we had always slept on together in our parents' home and cried out, "Why, oh why" I knew my so-called god would not be coming to comfort me.

But Jesus' cried as if he knew, REALLY KNEW that HIS God, whoever he is, could really feel his pain. I hope that when those women who loved him so are faced with their grief and despair in the days ahead, they will remember the example that their Jesus gave them. How freeing it must be to have a God who understands and cares about personal pain. Who even seems to feel it with you.

And then, I heard one of the women near me, I think her name was Salome, ask the others, "Did you hear what he said? Why he is singing one of David's songs? He is worshiping Yahweh, even as he dies. What can this mean?" And I am not ashamed to say that, by this time, I felt so much a part of their sisterhood that I leaned in – just like I was one of them – to hear the rest.

It seems Jesus words came from an ancient hymn that he probably learned from his Rabbi. From what I could tell, King David sang these very words when he himself had been treated with hostility and suffered at the hands of ***his*** own people. The women told how their sons and brothers, James and Peter and Lazarus, would come home from Sabbath School and talked about the King who prayed for deliverance and about how their God had saved him. They remembered that, just after he sang the words that Jesus cried, he also sang words of delivery and of his assurance that God never forsakes those whom he loves.

And this gave the women around me such joy, such peace. Some of them claimed that they had even sung the song after their Passover meal, just yesterday and knew it well. They said to one another, "See our God has not forsaken us. Our Jesus only wants to reassure us that we can say anything to our Heavenly Father, and we will understand."

The rest of the mob didn't know how to react. Some thought Elijah had been raised from the dead. Others rushed to give him wine on a sponge, lifting it to his mouth on a stick. But at that very moment Jesus took one last breath. And he simply died. Right then. And I knew in my heart at that moment that this man truly was the Messiah.

You see, my husband has witnessed many crucifixions and told me in great detail about them afterwards. And I know that often, it takes criminals days to die. The sun will set and rise and set again and still they get no relief from their agony. Yet Jesus lasted only a few hours. He said what he had to say to his tormentors, to his loved ones and to his God and then he simply gave up his Spirit.

And before I could begin to doubt my beliefs, we heard a loud sound – a surreal noise like a long, exaggerated clap of thunder. And they say that the curtain that hung at the altar in the Temple of David simply tore itself in two, like the hearts of those around me. And then there was silence because ***everyone*** knew. They knew that this man was not an ordinary man. And that perhaps, we had all been part of something horrific.

But one centurion, one brave man, a man I know well – my own Marcus, stepped away from his soldiers and toward the one who had finally received his peace. And without hesitation he said with authority to everyone who would listen, "Truly this man was God's Son!"

And that night, in our home, when we got the children to bed and the servants had left, we fell into each other's arms. And for the first time in many years, Marcus, my brave soldier, my beloved husband, wept.

*Please pray with me: Forgive me, Lord, for the times I – like those who stood at your cross – have acted with cruelty. Thank you for identifying, by your suffering, with all who ever feel forsaken or cry out, "Why?" Help me trust in you in my own times of adversity. Amen. *

*This closing prayer was taken from Final Words from the Cross written by Adam Hamilton. Abingdon Press, 2011, page 82.

A Word from the Cross: Hope

2 Corinthians 5:16-19(a); Luke 23:32, 39-43

Luke has long been my favorite Gospel because in it, Jesus is always concerned with the least and the lost. Since most of us have been lost a time or two in life, it is comforting to know that Jesus will seek us when we forget to seek him. Of course, Jesus' inclusion of all people in his healing and compassion did not sit well with the Pharisees, the religious leaders of Jesus' own people, because they only saw the world in black and white. Much to their dismay, Jesus saw the world in all of the glorious color that God created it with.

Because of his vision, Jesus allowed a prostitute to wash his feet. He saw only the love that she was pouring out on him in full view and not the sins she committed in the dark. Jesus ate with Zacchaeus, a hated tax collector and crook. He saw his potential for right living and recognized him as a child of Abraham, not just as one who was hopelessly lost. Jesus made a hated Samaritan the hero of his most well-known parable so we would know for years to come that God created ALL people in God's image. Not just the ones who look, think, talk and dress like we do.

In view of the way that Jesus lived, we should almost expect to read that he died the same way – with sinners. In fact, when Jesus preached his first sermon to the folks in his hometown of Nazareth, he stated very clearly that his MISSION, his purpose for living, was to set the oppressed free and preach good news to the captives. Clearly, Jesus came to seek and to save the lost.

So as we continue to listen to Jesus' last words from the cross, it should be no surprise that he turned to one of the criminals hanging with him and offered this hope: "Truly I tell you, today you will be with me in Paradise." In keeping with his purpose for living among us, instead of speaking these words of promise to the followers who had stayed with him all the way to the cross, he offered them to one ***we*** would consider the most undeserving person there. A criminal.

While it is translated into English as simply "criminal", the word in Greek really means "insurrectionist" or "political adversary". In other words, this guy hanging with Jesus didn't just steal a few goats or even murder his wife in a jealous rage. He was probably what we would call today a "terrorist". Picture Jesus on the cross with the man in London who drove his car into pedestrians on Westminster Bridge Wednesday, killing 5 people and wounding many others.

Yes, friends, it was THIS kind of criminal that Jesus offered hope to right before his death. And this doesn't sit well with us religious types who have worked hard all our lives to follow the rules, offer our best and lead lives of love. So what does the hope that Jesus offered this criminal right before he died teach ***us*** as his modern-day disciples?

The most obvious lesson is that it is never too late to recognize Christ as your Savior. And once you do, your past doesn't matter. The slate is wiped clean. Think about Paul. Born Saul of Tarsus, a Pharisee and therefore a bitter enemy of Jesus, he was known as one of the harshest critics of Christ and his followers in the early church. Yet, his personal encounter with Christ AFTER Jesus' resurrection made him such a new man that even his name changed, and he became Paul. And as a result, God called him specifically to share the Good News of Christ's life, death and resurrection with the Gentiles, the foreigners, the others. And Paul is also the author of much of our New Testament.

Indeed it was Paul's experience that it is never too late to be transformed by the love of Christ that led him to write in the passage that we just heard that being IN CHRIST makes us a new creation. Completely changed. Jesus was saying very plainly to this criminal that, even though he had made terrible decisions in his life that led to the pain and suffering of many people, it was not too late to be changed by God's grace. On the cross, listening to Jesus, the man realized his failure in life and accepted his imminent death by being repentant. And the hope that he died with was the promise of NEW life in Paradise with God. The chance to become a new creation.

Of course, you and I would NEVER make this offer to someone who is so undeserving. But maybe that is another reason that Jesus gave this hope to the criminal that he was dying with. To remind us that WE do not get to judge. In Jesus' day people who were religious did not even associate with people who weren't. His example on the cross planted the seed with his followers that it was going to be up to THEM to continue building the Kingdom of God when he left them. It also taught them how deep and high and wide the kingdom could be, that God alone would judge who is worthy. But it leaves a few questions for us.

For example, do people who are "unchurched" feel safe when they enter our sanctuary? Does everyone here feel accepted?

Do we value each other simply because we are children of God and not because of what we do? These are the last questions that Christ wanted to impress on his followers before he left us.

Of course, anytime we read this story, we have to wonder exactly what Jesus meant by Paradise? Knowing that Jesus is about to die, we interpret these words as a promise of being in Heaven. But perhaps Jesus was just inviting this criminal into the Kingdom of God right then. You see, I believe the kingdom of God is not so much a place as it is a condition. Because as soon as a child of God enters a relationship with God in Christ, that child has already entered Paradise. The healing, forgiveness, acceptance and love that every human being needs in order to thrive is ours the very moment we claim Christ as our Lord. The hope of being a new creation becomes more of a reality every time we accept the hand that Christ offers us.

Over the years, many ministers have used this passage to reassure those who have lost a loved one that, in some way we cannot understand, those who die in Christ go immediately to be with him. I myself have quoted it to families who were grieving and questioning where their loved one has gone. And I DO believe when we die in Christ, that we are received into his presence in some mysterious way. But perhaps Jesus is also saying that we don't have to wait until death to experience Paradise. Knowing that God is present with us - through the power and comfort of the Holy Spirit in every situation in life - is a hope that we can experience even before we get to Heaven.

But I believe that the real reason that Jesus offered this word to the criminal was to remind US of OUR mission. As I said Jesus LIVED his mission and DIED his mission, but he has only ***US*** to carry out that mission in the earthly kingdom now that he is in God's Heavenly kingdom. And this word, like all the others that we have read so far, tells us that we are to offer grace whenever we get the chance. Because every word spoken on the cross, indeed Jesus' entire mission can be summed up in that one word. Grace.

Sometimes I wonder if grace is one of the words we church people use so often that we have forgotten what it really means. Oh, we have a lot of acronyms for it – things like God's Riches at Christ's Expense or that Grace is God giving us what we don't deserve. And it is fine to remember it that way. But one of the pivotal moments in my seminary career was the day my Christian Education professor simply stopped in the middle of a sentence and exclaimed: "Grace is God looking at you and me and seeing Jesus Christ!" It was the first time in my life that the word grace had real meaning to me. What hope she gave me that day! And it is a hope that I cling to often.

In the same way, Jesus looked at the man whose life had been wasted with hatred and cruelty and saw a piece of himself inside of that man's heart. And when he did, he responded by reaching out and inviting him to repent and spend the rest of time in Eternity. And friends, the grace that our Savior gave us all on the cross is the word of hope that we are all called to share.

Because not only did he extend grace to the criminal, but he modeled it to us. He taught us how to give hope to others. Jesus Christ sees himself in EVERY man, woman and child and offers them the chance to become new creations. And so can we! Can you see Jesus Christ in your husband or daughter? It is likely you can, at least on most days. But can you see Jesus Christ in the thoughtless teenager who wounded your son's ego or the boss who gave you the pink slip? Or the soccer coach that didn't pick you for the team? Or the jerk that cuts you off in traffic? Jesus does.

And not only does he see himself in each of us, but he calls us to share the hope that is offered by his vision so that more and more people can live as new creations in Christ. So He asks us to see Him in every person we meet AND even in ourselves! I'd like to share a story of how hope can help us feel God in the midst of our struggles when the grace of Christ is shared.

One of the greatest privileges of being a pastor is being with someone when they die in Christ. That probably sounds really weird to most of you, but to be called to walk with one of God's children as they step from one kingdom into the next is simply a gift. I have been with people who had peaceful deaths and very painful ones as well, but the moment they enter the paradise of God, there is an instant sense of serenity that the chaos of life rarely gives us.

When I was serving as Chaplain at the Presbyterian Community, I was called in the middle of the night because a resident who had no family and was on Hospice felt sure that she was going to die. I assumed that she just didn't want to die with a stranger. So I got out of my warm bed and drove in the rain at 3:00 in the morning to be with God's child, whom I'll call Ruth.

Ruth had been in church all of her life. She knew the stories of grace that are found in the Bible. She still attended Worship when she could. Ruth was very smart and well read. I always assumed that her faith was secure. But when I entered her room, she asked the nurse to leave and had me pull my chair very close to her bed. Then she said, "I have done some terrible things in my life." I assured her that I had too, but she wanted to tell me about them.

So I listened with love and patience as she spilled out all that was on her heart. Then she looked at me and said in barely a whisper, "I have asked God to forgive me." I replied immediately, "He did." Ruth opened her eyes with such amazement and said, "Already?" And I assured her, "Already". And the tears began to roll out of the corner of her eyes when she understood that the love of God could not keep God from seeing Christ even in the heart of her sinfulness.

Today, this minute, you and I are living in God's kingdom. We are experiencing God's grace with every breath. We are already dwelling in God's paradise. May it be our mission to live with hope and see Jesus Christ in every person that crosses our path. And may we share this word of hope to each lost child of God that is found. You are forgiven. Already! In the name of the Father and of the Son and of the Holy Spirit. Amen.

A Word from the Cross: Covenant

Isaiah 41:17-20; John 19:28,29

As we come to the sixth word from Jesus on the cross, I will remind you that the previous words that have been spoken were words given to us in grace. A word of forgiveness; a word to teach us how to build community after Jesus left us; words of hope, trust and understanding. At first glance, Jesus' cry about his thirst seems to be the only word truly spoken out of his own need. A rare moment of self-centeredness.

But have ***you*** ever been thirsty? Of course, you have. Well try to remember the time that you wanted water more than anything in your life. It may have been on the opening day of a Clemson (or South Carolina) football season, where the Labor Day humidity combined with the excitement of the long day, has your throat completely parched. Or after a long hike in the mountains, when your water bottle has been dry during the last mile. Or after finishing a marathon or 5K run for your favorite charity.

In 2008, my husband and I were blessed to visit the Holy Land, including a side trip to the lost city of Petra in Jordan. The average temperature in May is only in the mid '80's but the area is 90% desert. The whole city is built out of sandstone and is located deep within a canyon of hills. The only way to get in is to walk, down a seemingly gentle slope. It is so dusty and dry that we were told to wear really old shoes and clothes that we didn't care about. I actually ended up throwing my shirt away!

After spending all day in this amazing, forgotten city, climbing up dusty pathways into the monastery, ruins of homes, and the steps of the amphitheater **AND** riding a camel, it was time to leave. Well friends that is when we found out that the gentle slope that we walked in on was not so gentle walking out. The best way to ascend was to zigzag the road. And it was only the promise of the little convenience store at the top of the hill that sold COLD water bottles that got me out!

But this would have been nothing compared to the thirst that Jesus experienced as he hung on the cross, broken and bleeding on our behalf. However, it is really important for us to understand the context that John wrote his Gospel in to discover what Jesus meant when he offered this, "I am thirsty!"

John states that Jesus made the cry "I am thirsty" to fulfill the Scriptures, and that is true. In Psalm 69, Kind David says about the enemies that are pursuing him: "I am weary with my crying; my throat is parched. My eyes grow dim with waiting for my God. They gave me poison for food, and for my thirst they gave me vinegar to drink." All good Jews standing at the foot of the cross would have known the source of these words and that God had rescued David.

But as I said, let's look at the context of the whole gospel of John. Most scholars believe, as I do, that John was the only Gospel writer who gave an eyewitness account of Jesus' life on earth. And in this matter of thirst, his account of Jesus' death is completely different from the other Gospels. Matthew, Mark and Luke have Jesus being offered the wine on a sponge in a taunting way but refusing it. But only John has Jesus ask for it.

Children of Yahweh would have known well the passage in Isaiah that we just heard that was delivered to the Exiles in Babylon. They were spoken to remind God's chosen people of the covenant that God had made with their ancestors. God made this promise to the people of Abraham, Isaac and Jacob many years earlier: "I will be your God and you will be my people."

Isaiah reminded the children of God that we are ***still*** covenant people by telling them, "When the poor and needy seek water, and there is none, and their tongue is parched with thirst, I the LORD will answer them." And because John wrote his Gospel about 70 years AFTER Jesus' death and resurrection, people had started to forget what Jesus had promised. They may not have been feeling the presence of the Holy Spirit among the persecution that they faced in the new church. They, too, may have forgotten that they were covenant people!

So John reminded them that HIS PERSONAL MEMORY was of Jesus repeating the words, "I thirst" so they would recall that Yahweh did not abandoned his children in Babylon. And God would not abandon them in Jerusalem so that they could believe and spread the Good News of grace with God's help. God was still present in the newly formed church, helping them tell others what it means to be covered by this covenant.

In the same way, God has not abandoned us. So when we turn on the news and hear of another senseless shooting in a nightclub, we can say, "I thirst for people to seek peaceful ways to disagree rather than simply reaching for a gun." When we read of the tragic deaths of 13 people on a church bus because the young person driving the pickup truck that hit them head on was texting while driving, we can say, "I thirst for people to truly value life. Help us value life as well." And we can be assured that God still honors the covenant made to us all, even when God seems absent. Remembering how long God has kept the covenant gives us hope that we are STILL God's people.

So while we live among thoughtlessness, violence, hunger, homelessness, addiction and other struggles, Jesus' word, "I thirst" encourages ***us*** to keep on thirsting for righteousness and goodness. And the reminder that we are covenant people gives us hope for the day when God's kingdom really will come and God's will can be done, as we pray for each week in the Lord's Prayer.

Another detail that John gives us in his account that reminds us of our gifts as covenant people is that he makes a point to tell us that the wine offered to Jesus on a sponge was lifted to his mouth on a branch of hyssop. Now in reality, hyssop is a small, bushy plant and it would be almost impossible to attach a sponge to it, so it is more likely that the sponge was on a stick as the other Gospels tell us.

But I believe John ***reported*** that it was a hyssop branch because, as believers in the new church made up of Jews and Christians, his audience would again have understood the significance and promise that it represented. According to John's Gospel, Jesus was crucified during Passover. The Jews at the cross would have just reenacted the defining moment in their history when the angel of death killed the firstborn in every Egyptian household but "passed over" the Hebrew homes because of the blood on their doorpost.

The writer of Exodus tells us that each Hebrew was to take the blood of an unblemished lamb that had been sacrificed to God, dip in it a HYSSOP branch and shake the blood on the doorpost to keep the covenant people within the house safe. And speaking of sacrifice, in the Old Testament we read that the priests took hyssop and dipped it into water, sometimes mixed with blood or ashes to purify someone who had been cleansed of sin. John's words emphasize not only Jesus' physical thirst but our Spiritual thirst for the kind of cleansing that only God can give.

But the strongest reminder that this word from Jesus was a symbol of our covenant status is that ONLY in John's Gospel is Jesus referred to as "The Lamb of God." In the Old Testament, the Hebrews were asked to sacrifice unblemished lambs on the altar to atone for their sins. ONLY JOHN'S GOSPEL makes the point that Jesus' death takes place while the lambs were being slaughtered at the Temple. In this way, he reminds us that Jesus is the Lamb of God and the New Covenant as well. Because Jesus thirsted for God's will to be done, we do not have to bring little animals to church each week to atone for everything we have done wrong since last Sunday. When Jesus entered the arms of his Father after his death, God exclaimed, "Finally, a sacrifice that is acceptable."

That is why I planned for us to hear this word from Jesus, "I am thirsty" on the day when we observe the Lord's Supper. Jesus Christ IS our New Covenant. His blood was shed on the cross in pain and suffering because God knows that, after every opportunity that his children have been given to live up to the Covenant, we cannot. We have learned in Confirmation Class that God made a covenant with Moses. He said to Moses on Mt. Sinai when the Law was given, "Now, if you obey me completely and keep my covenant, you will be my treasured possession among all peoples, though all the earth is mine" (Exodus 19:5).

But try as we might, you and I cannot keep that Covenant. We do not honor the Sabbath. We do not always honor our parents. While we try to speak the truth with our lips, we often lie with our hearts. We steal in ways that we do not mean to and covet our friend's younger body, naturally curly hair, bigger house and faster car. And we just can't help ourselves because we are merely human.

But in spite of our sins, God loves us. God loves YOU and ME. God WANTS to spend eternity in our presence. And so recognizing the faults of the first covenant, he let his Son thirst on the cross for the righteousness and obedience that would pave the way to our salvation. The very human Jesus thirsted because of our sinfulness and the Divine Jesus offered his own blood to quench our thirst.

So as we come to the Table today, remember the covenant. And remember the cost. Because every sin, every thoughtless act or intentional transgression. Every forbidden fruit that we have tasted and every prayer that we have offered to be better than we are but have not been able to achieve on our own, has been covered in the blood of our Risen Savior. And the thirst of God the Father, Son and Holy Spirit has been quenched for all time. Amen.

A Word from the Cross: Victory!

John 20:1-10; John 19:28-30

For those of you who are visitors today, I will tell you that during Lent, we examined what is commonly known as "The Seven Last Words of Jesus from the Cross." These are the seven phrases that Christ uttered during the crucifixion. We have learned that even the words that seem to be for him were really for us, offered to teach us one last lesson or to extend one more bit of grace before his death. Each week the sermon here was entitled: "A Word from the Cross" with a key word that hopefully captured the meaning of that phrase.

But I am wondering if any of you who are not visitors and ***heard*** the sermons noticed that I only preached on six of those words. If you didn't notice or perhaps just didn't count, you are probably wondering if I have missed the boat, fallen asleep or am simply not paying attention. You're thinking that you just heard me say that the stone was rolled away! Jesus Christ is NOT in the tomb; the disciples did NOT find him there. So you may be asking yourselves, "Why is Julie taking us back to the cross?"

Well, first let me say that the fact that the tomb could not hold our Lord is THE GOOD NEWS for Christians of all ages. But as I planned my sermons throughout our Lenten journey, I withheld this last word for a reason. Namely this - it is so hard to decide what to ***SAY*** about Easter that everyone hasn't already heard. In fact, I told someone that my sermon today was going to be, "The stone was rolled away. The tomb was empty. He is risen! Enjoy your ham!" But of course, THAT would NEVER do.

However, while studying these beautiful gifts from Jesus on the cross, the Holy Spirit urged me to hold on to this last word just for this morning. "It is finished!" Because as Easter people, who live on *this* side of the cross, this may be the best news of all, when you think of all the things that **"IT"** can stand for.

When Christ cried out, "It is finished", it is recorded in the English language as three separate words but in the original Greek that John wrote in, Jesus spoke only one word. So to translate it as "finished" is *adequate* but does not really give us a full appreciation for what it was that was accomplished on the cross. In my Greek dictionary, I counted no less than twelve definitions for the word including "complete", "execute", "accomplish", "fill up" and "pay". But James Montgomery Boice explained it best when he wrote that this word from Jesus on the cross was a complete summation of the gospel!

So let us consider that "it" stood for Jesus' suffering. Surely Jesus knew that never again would he be spit upon by Roman soldiers or have his motives questioned by Pharisees and Sadducees. He would endure no more flogging or mocking or betrayal by his followers. No desertion from his disciples and denial from his close friends. No one ever suffered as Jesus did and surely, he knew that he was finally headed to a place of eternal rest and that the sufferings of life were finished. But can we take "IT" a step further and believe that OUR suffering has ended too? Well, yes, I think we can.

You see, the idea that suffering can have an ending is an important word to anyone who is living in what I call a Good Friday day. Often when we get bad news – when the test comes back positive or pink slip is delivered or the crops fail or the stock market plummets, it is easy to think OUR lives are finished and suffering is all that lies ahead. Jesus' ability to pronounce suffering finished on that day gives us hope that Sunday will come again in our lives when we believe in the sacrifices that Christ made on our behalf. So this means that ULTIMATELY our suffering will end too.

Or perhaps, Jesus was saying these words for the benefit of the doubting Jews in the crowd so that they would understand that "it" stood for the prophecies of the coming Messiah. We know that most of Jesus' Jewish opponents were very pious and so they would have known the Scriptures well. And in many ways, his proclamation was almost a summation of what their prophets had been telling them for centuries.

Isaiah had foretold that the Messiah would be born of a woman without benefit of a human father and that he would be rejected by his own people. As rejection stood embodied around the cross in the very ones who had yelled, "Crucify Him!" perhaps these words of the prophet rang in their ears. Isaiah had also said that the Messiah would open the eyes of the blind, unstop the ears of the deaf and make the lame to leap like deer. Witnesses to his many miracles would have known that these words had come true.

Micah had said that the savior would be born in Bethlehem. Zechariah had predicted that the Messiah would ride into Jerusalem on the back of a donkey and the Psalmist had written that his hands and feet would be pierced and that soldiers would cast lots for his clothing. So as both his followers and enemies gathered to watch his death, they may have been remembering the words from their OWN Scriptures that had been taught to them all their lives and realized that "IT" was the fulfillment of the Old Testament Messianic promise.

Of course, the whole realm of our Christian doctrine is based on the belief that, upon Jesus death, SIN is finished, and I am sure that this was on the mind of Christ that day too. His death means the end of *our* sins and that sin is not ON us anymore. Now, please notice that I did not say that sin is not IN us. We will always be sinful in nature because of the fall of Adam. Of course, some people have a hard time understanding the true implications of their sinfulness. A Sunday School teacher once asked her middle school class if they knew what sins of omission were. After some thought, one young man answered, "They're the sins we should have committed but haven't gotten around to."

But when we are honest, we recognize our sinfulness. And we know that our hope is in the knowledge that by Christ's atoning death on the cross, sin cannot be ON us. Your guilt and mine were transferred to a Holy substitute. As Reformed Christians, we believe that there is nothing we can do to take away our sin. No rosary prayers, no little animals burned at the altar. Left to our own devices we will always live mired down IN sin until after our death. But by the sacrifice of his only son, God has taken any sin that is ON us and transferred it to His own child. So in effect, the cross of Christ has become the GRAVE for our sins. And there is nothing WE can do to remove our sinfulness except believe! And so, IT, sin, has spoken for the last time.

Of course, Jesus could easily have meant "my work" is finished! Jesus had been telling people over and over that *his* work was to glorify God and bring back the lost sheep of Israel to their covenantal father. Earlier in the priestly prayer that John recorded Jesus to have prayed he said to God, "I have brought you glory on earth by completing the work you gave me to do." So now, having reassured God that his work was done, maybe he wanted his people to hear it too. So he proclaimed, "I can do no more for you than what I have already done. IT IS FINISHED!"

At this point, I would like to say that I do NOT believe that "it" means OUR work is finished. Now for those of us real "Type A" personalities, this is a huge relief because we cannot relate to the idea of having nothing to do! I was driving through the country the other day and passed a little non-denominational church with a marquee out front that said, "God so loved the world that he did not send a committee!" Some of us diehard Presbyterians may not know how to act if we get to Heaven and don't have a committee meeting to go to.

However, by the fact that all four gospel accounts of the resurrection of Christ include some form of the words, "GO AND TELL", we know that while Christ's work may be finished, ours is not. When Michelangelo put the finishing touches on the Sistine Chapel, I can imagine that, as the artist, he leaned back, looked with satisfaction at his work and declared, "I can do no more." And so Jesus, as the master himself, could declare on the cross that with his death, he TOO, could do no more.

But as recipients of the masterpiece of eternal life, our work is not finished. We, like the first disciples at the tomb, are commanded by our Lord to go and tell. To teach and preach and baptize even to the ends of the earth. To share the good news of God's love and grace with anyone who will listen. And to demonstrate it in our daily living.

But I believe that the true meaning to us on this Easter day, the word of resurrection that we find in this last battle cry of Christ from the cross is the assurance that "DEATH" is finished. Because THAT really is **the** Gospel. And I feel sure that THIS is why the Holy Spirit kept sending this Good Friday word into my thoughts for Easter Sunday.

As much as I try to keep an open mind and accept other ideas and viewpoints, I have a very traditional idea of what happened when Jesus was taken off the cross. I believe that when Jesus' spirit departed that day and they laid him in the tomb, that he literally went to Hell on our behalf and did a three-day battle with the devil. And by the appearance of the resurrected Christ to so many people, we know that Jesus Christ was the final victor.

So when Jesus cried those words on the cross, he gave us the message of resurrection and new life. He gave us in that ONE word a picture of the Holy city where, as the old song says, "all who would might enter and no one be denied." On the cross on Good Friday, Jesus have us hope and light and joy and life in that word given in sacrificial love. And so, the joy of our

Easter this day is that when Jesus said, "It is finished!" what he means was that your eternal life and mine had just begun. The word from the cross is VICTORY.

I don't mean to paint a rosy picture of a perfect life for all who believe. Everyone here knows that this is not true. But I do believe the story of the cross and the empty tomb is truly the story of the grace to cope with *what is* and the story of hope for *what is to come*. Christ's sacrifice on the cross gives us this gift and calls us to hold on to it every day. So today, as we go from this place, let us each in our own way go and tell the good news that it is finished. Alleluia! Amen.

More Than Chocolate

More Than Chocolate

More than Chocolate: Giving up Control

Genesis 2:15-17, 3:1-7; Matthew 4:1-11

As I mentioned during the Ash Wednesday service this week, Presbyterians do not generally "give up" something for Lent. In fact, I usually prefer to take something on during Lent such as an intentional time of prayer, reading through one of the Gospels or taking on a mission project. But the Holy Spirit gave me the idea that there ***are*** certain things that we all need to give up in our lives that may have a greater impact on us than abstaining from French fries or wine. Things that pertain to our spiritual and emotional health more than our bodily health.

So for the Sundays of Lent, I will be preaching sermons on things we ***all*** might consider giving up. The series "More Than Chocolate" will be geared towards things that are obstacles that many of us face that prevent us from living into the faith and the discipleship that God desires for all of his children.

The passages that we heard this morning are both stories of beginnings. The story of Adam and Eve is not only where God begins with humankind but also where humankind first begins to live outside the will of our Heavenly father.

Our secretary's 4-year-old grandson Ty, out of the clear blue this week said to his dad, "I sure am glad Adam and Eve sinned!" When he asked him why Ty replied, "If they hadn't, we would all be running around naked!" Of course, Ty was referring to the fact that God sewed fig leaves to cover Adam and Eve because once they had eaten the forbidden fruit, their eyes were opened, and they recognized their nakedness. This is actually considered the first act of grace by our Lord recorded in the Bible.

Now theologically, this story is about the way the sin entered into Creation. But I am not sure examining this story from a theological perspective is what we need to hear during Lent. As a minister, I cannot tell you how many times I have been asked things like, "If God loves us, why did he create the serpent in the first place?" Or "where did the snake come from?" We all know that the answer to the question of the origin of sin is a lot longer than my average 6- or 7-page sermon. But as the suggested reading for the first Sunday of Lent, the story does speak to the issue of giving up control. And our need to be in control might well be something that keeps us from living within the will of God.

Anyone who has been to Vacation Bible School knows that Adam and Eve were the first people created by God – the beginning of humanity. We also know that God created the garden for Adam and Eve to live in and that it was full of "every tree that is pleasant to the sight and good for food". The writer of Genesis tells us that God put humankind in the garden to "keep and till it". Actually, in the original Hebrew we are told that Adam is to "settle down" on the ground and serve and keep it. God needed someone to help take care of creation and God would take care of humankind.

Of course, there was one – ONLY ONE – restriction. Although God gave Adam and Eve dominion over all the earth, more intelligence than anything else he had created and the ability to communicate and understand in ways that the other creatures did not, God ***did*** ask that they not eat from the tree of the knowledge of good and evil. That was it! One law to follow. Just don't try to be me!

Of course, there is one more important factor that is not spelled out so clearly in the creation story in Genesis. That is: God gave humankind freewill. God loves us too much to treat us like puppets on a string, going through life simply as actors on a stage. God gives us the freedom to choose to be obedient or not. And it is the "not" that got Adam and Eve in trouble and that gets us in trouble every time.

The simple fact of the matter is that God offered Adam and Eve a lot of freedom but from where we sit today, it is easy to see that they wanted to be in complete control. They wanted to be ***like*** God – to see things the way God sees them. No, I will go a step further and say that they wanted to BE God, not just ***like*** God. And when the serpent seemed to offer a logical way for Adam and Eve to be like God, to know what God knows, to see what God sees the way God sees it – well, they bit, to make an awful pun! And that is because they did not trust in God's plan. And friends, the opposite of control is trust.

Many of us have good reason to be distrustful – we have been hurt, we have been taken advantage of, we have not been allowed to live up to our potential because someone has gotten in our way or circumstances have not been in our favor. But at some time or another, if we are going to choose happiness, choose joy, indeed choose life, we are going to have to trust someone about some things. And why not start with God? A friend of mine, who clearly has a lot more self-confidence than many of us, told me yesterday. "When I think that God created me in His image, I think that He has made something pretty wonderful, so I will just let God follow out his plan for me." So giving up control is not about being willing to be taken advantage of. It is letting God work out God's plan for every life here without interference with our human ideas of what is right.

So now let's go to that other story of beginnings. The beginning of Jesus' public ministry. Matthew tells us the Holy Spirit broke through the clouds at Jesus' baptism and declared him to be the beloved Son of God. Yet, that ***same*** Spirit led him into the wilderness for forty days and nights of temptation.

And while Jesus is out in the wilderness fasting for forty days, good old Satan appears and offers him the chance to grab the reign of power. And we see that some things never change. That crafty old serpent had a one-track mind. To tempt humankind with power! It worked on Adam and Eve, but would it work on Jesus?

His first try was this: If you are the Son of God, command these stones to become bread." Satan thinks that he can use the same powers of persuasion that he did with Eve, tempting Jesus with something delicious and pleasing to his sight to succeed in having him trust his own needs rather than depend on God.

Of course, Matthew has stated the obvious – that after forty days and nights with no food, Jesus is famished. So Satan points out how easy it would be for him to perform a miracle and satisfy his own needs. To turn the stones into bread. Satan knows that if Jesus is tricked into using his miraculous power that the battle is over, for Jesus will have responded as God and not as man, by turning the rocks into bread.

Jesus the man wants and needs bread and Satan knows this. But Jesus the Son of God refuses to use his divine power and instead responds with the true bread of life which is God's word. Jesus gives up his ability to control and instead trusts in the plan that God has for his life.

"Man does not live on bread alone, but on every word that comes from the mouth of God". (Deut 8:3). Jesus responded to temptation in a way that Eve did not. Jesus quotes God's word exactly and uses it, not as an explanation, but as a basis for living a life true to God's will. Jesus wins this first battle and we learn that, in order to overcome the desires of the flesh and our human need to be in control, we must use God's word as a weapon that will help us trust in God's direction for our lives.

When Satan realizes that Jesus will continue to trust in God's word, he also realizes that that Jesus has completely entrusted His life into His Father's hands. So Satan decides to whisk him away to Jerusalem, on top of God's Temple. There he takes his cues from Jesus and HE uses God's word to try to break him. One might paraphrase Satan's second temptation in this way:

"So, you have entrusted your life to God, have you? That's good. I can see that you really are a man of faith. You trust in God and in His Word. That, too, is good. So let me call your attention to some words of Scripture that may be really important right now."

Satan then quotes Psalm 91 to suggest that if Jesus throws himself from a high place, God's angels will come to the rescue. He even takes him to the place where many believed that God actually lived at that time – the Temple. From Satan's grasp of what Jesus had already spoken, he felt that this temptation would work: Jesus should prove His faith in God, and in God's Word, by leaping from the pinnacle of the temple. If He was God's Son, surely God would save Him, especially right there where God chose to abide. So how could Jesus resist?

Satan may also have seen this temptation as a win/win situation. If Jesus jumped from the Temple and Satan was successful in keeping the angels from rescuing Jesus, then he would be dead, and Satan would be the victor. But if Jesus jumped from the temple and God used His angels to rescue Him, then Satan would have succeeded in prompting Jesus to act in a way that showed that he did not trust God so much after all. Jesus would have been choosing to be in control rather than to let God have control. Of course, Jesus did not fall for Satan's trickery, as Eve did.

Then Satan tempted Jesus with control over all the kingdoms of the world. Yet even though he was only beginning his ministry, Jesus knew that his mission was to gather all the nations into the kingdom of God. Satan tempted him to take a short cut to God's purpose, again to take control rather than trust in God. Jesus knew that his work involved the crucifixion – the shedding of his blood to cover our sins.

Christ's response showed his true allegiance. Clearly, he would not serve the devil for any reason – even if it seemed to line up with something easier – Jesus proved to Satan that it is better to trust God's plan ***and*** God's methods.

Now all of this preaches very nicely doesn't it? Good break down of the Scripture, righteous thinking and all that. But friends, I sat in the pews a lot longer than I have been standing behind the pulpit. And if I were in the pews right now, I might be thinking, "Well of course ***Jesus*** let God be in control, HE'S JESUS after all!" But what about me?

Now subconsciously, I chose control as the first thing to give up for Lent because it is so hard for me to let others be in control. I like to drive when I go places. I like to be on the winning team. I like to think that my plan is the best. And to "let go and let God" sounds a little to me like checking my brain at the door.

But I have learned over time that letting God be in control does not mean sitting in the middle of a field and saying, "The Lord will provide." God gave each of us particular gifts and God is best served when we let ***God*** put those gifts to work in us. And letting God be in control of my life does not involve knowing every detail. It means acknowledging that God's plan for me is to have life and have it abundantly.

I used to struggle so much with that verse in the Psalms that says, "Be still and know that I am God." For years I convinced myself it was because I didn't like the "be still" part. I am high-functioning and work best under pressure. But I have finally had to admit that it is the "know that I am God" part that was hard for me. Letting God be God means letting God have dominion over EVERY aspect of my life. And that is hard. I finally started to like this verse when I heard it translated as: "Chill out – I got this one!"

Yet what better season than Lent, the season of repentance, to begin turning our lives and our wills over to the will of God? What better time is there to give up control and let God's will be done? What better time than Lent to really trust God?

There is a well know prayer that we call the "Serenity Prayer" that probably sums up what I have been saying much better than I can. Many of us know the beginning of the prayer but may not know that it was written by Reinhold Niebuhr, an American theologian and professor at a Presbyterian Seminary. And many of us do not know the whole prayer. Listen to it and think about all that is promised when we truly surrender to God's will, living each day under God's control. Letting God be God!

God grant me the serenity
To accept the things I cannot change;
Courage to change the things I can;
And wisdom to know the difference.

Living one day at a time;
Enjoying one moment at a time;
Accepting hardships as the pathway to peace;
Taking, as He did, this sinful world
As it is, not as I would have it;

Trusting that He will make all things right
If I surrender to His Will;
So that I may be reasonably happy in this life
And supremely happy with Him
Forever and ever in the next.

More than Chocolate: Giving Up Preconceived Notions

John 3:1-17

Some of you may be wondering what in the world I am talking about giving up this morning! So let me explain. I have found that often, I make up my mind about a person, a situation, a possibility or an expectation before I get all the evidence. I am going to a party with people who all live in that "ritzy" part of town and assume I will have a terrible time because there won't be one down-to-earth person that I can relate to. OR That woman cannot get her child to quit crying in the grocery store – why doesn't she just spank him – she must be a terrible parent. OR Everyone in the room is much smarter than I am, there is no way they will be able to relate to my idea, presentation, sermon, lesson or whatever. Are you following? Am I the only one here who suffers from this judgmental behavior?

Well, now that we have got that straight, let's talk about the text. There are many Bible verses and passages that have become popular in modern culture. But no single verse has impacted the world as much as John 3:16: "*For God so loved the world that he gave his one and only Son, that whoever believes in him shall not perish but have eternal life.*" Or, you may be more familiar with the King James translation: "*For God so loved the world, that he gave his only begotten Son, that whosoever believeth in him should not perish, but have everlasting life.*"

On the surface, one of the reasons John 3:16 has become so popular is that it represents a simple summary of a profound truth. In short, God loves the world, including people such as you and me. He wanted to save the world so desperately that He became part of the world in the form of a man -- Jesus Christ. He experienced death on the cross so that all people could enjoy the blessing of eternal life in heaven. That's the message of the gospel.

But for the purposes of Lent and our sermon series "More Than Chocolate" it's important for us to study these words in their context. Because many of us may assume that the verses before and after are not nearly as important – we may have a preconceived notion that we don't need to understand what led Jesus to offer these words of hope. And that is a notion that we need to give up!

This summary of God's truth is the result of a visit from Nicodemus to Jesus, a rabbi who has made a name for himself by the miracles that he has performed. Nicodemus is not only a Pharisee – that is an interpreter of the Law of Moses – but an elite member of the Sanhedrin, sort of the Jewish Supreme Court of the Day. And even though he recognizes that Jesus has certain powers that could only come from God, he is still not quite sure about who Jesus is. Nicodemus comes in the dark of night, presumably out of a concern for his own safety, to ask Jesus some questions that will help him clarify his mission.

Listen again to the beginning of their meeting, this time from Eugene Peterson's *The Message*. "There was a man of the Pharisee sect, Nicodemus, a prominent leader among the Jews. Late one night he visited Jesus and said, "Rabbi, we all know you're a teacher straight from God. No one could do all the

God-pointing, God-revealing acts you do if God weren't in on it."

Jesus said, "You're absolutely right. Take it from me: Unless a person is born from above, it's not possible to see what I'm pointing to—to God's kingdom." "How can anyone," said Nicodemus, "be born who has already been born and grown up? You can't re-enter your mother's womb and be born again. What are you saying with this 'born-from-above' talk?"

Now we can see several preconceived notions in just this portion of the conversation and indeed might have a few of our own. We might think that Nicodemus is a coward. But, after researching the passage, I don't think we should jump to this conclusion. As a Pharisee, he was part of an elite brotherhood that never included more than 6000 Jews in the whole world. When one was asked to join this brotherhood, he had to take a pledge in front of three witnesses that he would spend his whole life observing every detail of the Law, the most sacred thing in the Jewish world. To add or take away ONE WORD from the Law was considered a deadly sin.

On top of this, he was a member of the Sanhedrin, therefore he is supposed to understand everything. So to be seen asking Jesus, a novice rabbi, to explain some of his teachings, teachings that were based on God's word, would be like Chief Justice John Roberts asking a first-year law student to help him interpret a long-standing statute. If word got out that he had done this, his integrity would be in doubt, he would lose respect from his peers and those who looked to him for counsel and every ounce of credibility that he had earned that got him where he was would be stripped away.

It is easy to judge someone when you don't know all the circumstances. Like that woman in the grocery store. When a screaming child is getting on my last nerve, I have to remind myself that she has probably been in daycare all day, that she is tired and she is hungry and that her mother just wants to get something for supper so she can go home after working all day to cook, bathe children, help with homework and do laundry before collapsing into bed and starting the whole routine over tomorrow. So now, knowing more about what was at stake for Nicodemus, I am going to let that preconceived notion go.

In truth, Nicodemus was actually brave. He was risking a lot more than one would think at first glance in trying to discern if this really was the son of God. Then there was his preconceived notion about what it meant to be born again. But before we get to Nicodemus let's think about OUR OWN thoughts about the idea of being "born again". This notion might actually be a geographical one. I grew up in Greenville, SC – home to that very conservative, evangelical college that will not be named. As a young girl, it was not unusual for someone to walk up to on the streets and asked if I had been born again. And when this happened, I immediately put the questioner in the category of "religious fanatic". He or she belongs with the ones who hold the "John 3:16" signs up at an NFL game and people passing out tracts on salvation on Main Street.

Or not! Perhaps they have had a real call, just like I did, to bring the Good News of salvation to God's people. My call led me to seminary. Theirs led to street evangelism. Who am I to judge? But assuming that Nicodemus never categorized Jesus as a religious fanatic, then what is the issue here?

Nicodemus had a preconceived notion that Jesus meant he had to reenter his mother's womb. What Jesus what saying was something completely different. AND I think it is the same thing that was meant when I was faced with that question as a child.

Jesus is not suggesting that a grown person must experience literal birth. No, he was suggesting that Nicodemus' faith was incomplete. Maybe even immature. Even though he was a learned scholar and interpreter of the Law, he had not learned what to DO with his faith that would really help bring about the Kingdom of God. In fact, his coming to see Jesus in the dark speaks more about his childlike understanding of what it means to follow Yahweh than about his being afraid.

Nicodemus may have known the Law, but he didn't know how to use. So Jesus said to him and us, "You cannot live out your faith like you want to have the safety of your mother's womb – your faith is practically still in utero! If you were born again, you would know that you must declare your faith out in the light where others can see it and where it will have an impact on the kingdom".

I would suspect there are a few 21st Century Nicodemuses around. People who believe in Jesus, maybe even who are successful spiritual leaders within their faith community but want to keep their faith and their life separate. They will open the Bible Study with prayer but sure wouldn't stop their friends at the Piedmont Club from lifting their salad fork by offering to bless the lunch first. They have faith, like to think of themselves as faithful people, but don't want to let it change their life or interfere with what others expect from them.

Friends, with all that is going on in our world, our neighborhoods, our schools, even our churches, the last thing that God's kingdom needs is a bunch of lukewarm Christians who don't want to be accused of believing if it rocks someone's boat. Did you know that people during the Reformation who sympathized with the principles of the Reformers but were unwilling to publicly identify with them were known as "Nicodemites"?

Reading that reminded me of the time I had the opportunity to hear Genie Gamble, a minister that I have always admired, preach once at Montreat. She grew up in a family of lawyers and judges. In fact, she was considered a failure in her family because she only became a minister and author. And having grown up around legalese, she preached a sermon about how we can be a witness for Christ. I will always remember her words.

She said that, once someone knows you are a Christian, you become a witness for Christ whether you want to or not. And it is up to each of us to determine whether we will be CREDIBLE witnesses or INCREDIBLE ones. We can do that without falling into the category of being a religious fanatic, but we will have to experience new life and live it in every place and with all people for it to be REAL faith.

I know that we pray every Sunday in the Lord's Prayer, "Thy Kingdom come, Thy will be done." But I wonder if we really understand what we are asking for? As I have matured more in my own faith, I have come to believe that the kingdom of God is not so much a place but a condition. It is a society where God's will is as perfectly done on earth as it is in Heaven. If we really mean what we pray then we must be willing to be changed, right in the light, where everyone will notice! Our preconceived notions about what it means to be born again will have to be discarded so that we can live out our faith in a way that attracts people to God's kingdom.

Nicodemus had another preconceived notion that is all too common among us. In fact, it's one that we develop early in life, at about the age of two. It is the "I can do that all by myself!" syndrome. And it prevented him from understanding Jesus' born again talk. Nicodemus' questions to Jesus implied that he thought HE had to DO something to be born again. Well friends, who does all the work in childbirth? I don't need to get too graphic, but all a child has to do is be born. The mother does all the work! And all we have to do to be born again is believe. Because God does ALL the work.

Yet, we have been so conditioned to become independent, successful, self-reliant achievers that we often feel like failures if we have to ask for help. Nicodemus didn't want anyone to know he didn't understand everything. And when Jesus' metaphor of childbirth still left Nicodemus baffled, Jesus told him that the Spirit blows where it will. This means that the Holy Spirit of God will give us what we need when we need it. All we have to do is ask the Spirit to enter our lives. We must only be willing to truly live as Christ's disciples! And to give up the preconceived notion that there is something that we can do to save ourselves besides have faith. The problem for us is this: how do we recognize that Spirit? We might finally ask for God's help but how do we recognize God's answer?

Many of us can testify to the person whom God sends into our lives at just the moment when our self-reliance has caused us more harm than good. We can name the unexpected friend that almost came out of nowhere who finally makes life safe enough to trust with the secret we have born alone for years. We can recall the episode of "The Big Bang Theory" that helped us understand the coworker who always gets on our last nerve. Or the hymn that touches us so and leads us to finally open our hearts to the possibilities that God has been offering us for years, but that we were too proud to accept. The Spirit comes in many ways! God covets our closeness and wants us to come to Him with every need, question, joy and doubt.

So perhaps that last preconceived notion we need to give up during Lent is the one about how hard we have to work for everything. That is why Jesus gives Nicodemus this now famous verse: to remind us all that grace is free! God gives it to us out of love. We must work hard to learn, to provide for ourselves and our families, to grow in our relationships, including our faith relationship. But we do not have to birth ourselves!

In her sermon on this text, minister Debbie Blue reminds us of how hard God has worked, and still works, to bring you and me to fullness of life. God created us and has walked with us in sin and rejection. Finally, God took on human flesh. In Christ, God was born and suffered and ate and drank and laughed and died and lived again. In doing that, God forever cracked the barrier that stands between the human and the divine! God is in our lives and we are in God's life, and life can be new, filled with the joy and gladness of God's presence. This is God's gift to us in Jesus Christ. Life lived fully, without holding on to any baggage of what we don't understand or don't want to accept or are too afraid to truly claim. God give us life - life lived abundantly. Life lived now. This is the good news of the gospel. Amen.

More than Chocolate: Giving up Love with Limits

Mathew 5:38-48

My first thought when I read this passage, which is NOT the suggested reading for the day, by the way, was this: Oh, I get it – don't hit back, love your enemies, pray for those who do terrible things to you, love people who are unlovable and oh yes, be perfect! A really smart preacher would not CHOOSE to preach from this passage!

My second thought was Robert Fulghum's "Rules for living". You are all familiar with it but just in case you need a reminder, here it is in part. "All I really need to know about how to live and what to do and how to be I learned in kindergarten. Wisdom was not at the top of the graduate school mountain, but there in the sand pile at school. These are the things I learned: Share everything. Play fair. Don't hit people. Put things back where you found them. Clean up your own mess. Don't take things that aren't yours. Say you're sorry when you hurt somebody. Wash your hands before you eat. Flush. Warm cookies and cold milk are good for you. Live a balanced life - learn some and think some and draw and paint and sing and dance and play and work every day some. Take a nap every afternoon. When you go out in the world, watch out for traffic, hold hands and stick together. Everything you need to know is in there somewhere. The Golden Rule and love and basic sanitation. Ecology and politics and equality and sane living. Take any one of those items and extrapolate it into sophisticated adult terms and apply it to your family life or your work or government or your world and it holds true and clear and firm. Think what a better world it would be if we all - the whole world - had cookies and milk at about 3 o'clock in the afternoon and then lay down with our blankies for a nap. Or if all governments had as a basic policy to always put things back where they found them and to clean up their own mess. And it is still true, no matter how old you are, when you go out in the world, it is best to hold hands and stick together."

I guess when we put this portion of the Sermon on the Mount into kindergarten terms, it doesn't seem quite as daunting. But for the purposes of our Lenten Sermon Series "More than Chocolate" I think that Jesus is telling us that when we love without limits, we are like God. End of sermon, let's go to lunch, right? If only it were that easy!

In this text, there are two basic discipleship commitments that Jesus is asking each of us to make that I would like us to consider. The first is that we are called to waive our "rights". Please notice the air quotes when I said that. Because contrary to what most 21st Century Christians believe, we have no rights. Everything that we have is a gift from God. When Jesus called Peter, James, John, Vickie, Candy and Rick to be disciples, he did not promise anyone a world full of sunshine and rainbows. He said, "You have signed up to die to self". Being a disciple of Christ means giving up the right to live the way WE see fit and to live the way Jesus calls us to. Any benefit that goes along with that is purely grace.

Then Jesus gets specific. Now when Jesus began a sentence with "you have heard it said", the good Jews in the crowd knew that he was going to quote their Scriptures. True to form, Jesus offers the law of retaliation, found in at least three places in the Books of Moses. "An eye for an eye and a tooth for a tooth." Many of you have heard the quote attributed to Ghandi that if we followed this kind of thinking, the whole world blind. But that was not its original intent.

This law of retaliation actually sets restrictions on how we are to retaliate. In other words, if you knock out my tooth, I can knock out yours, but I cannot beat you to a pulp. You see, God gave this Law as an equalizer of justice. Because we all know that when we have been wronged, we want to line up forces, pull out all the stops and go for the jugular. But God said, "No – you can only retaliate by doing what was done to you." It is also important to understand that the law said that you COULD take an eye for an eye but not that you HAD to.

Now this sermon takes place early in Jesus' ministry, so his listeners may not have learned yet that when he says, "You have heard that it is said" that he follows with "But I say to you". However, you and I know that Jesus is going to offer an alternative way of doing things.

Jesus says we CAN retaliate according to the Law of Moses, but we can also choose not to. He tells us to be perfect, just as our Father in Heaven is perfect. Which of course sounds impossible. But how about this? "When you give up love with limits, you are like God."

Jesus then give four examples of what it means not to retaliate against an evil person. If anyone strikes you on the right cheek, turn the other also; if anyone wants to sue you and take your coat, give your cloak as well; if anyone forces you to go one mile, go also the second mile. Give to everyone who begs from you, and do not refuse anyone who wants to borrow from you.

These four illustrations all involve laws that were specifically applicable to the culture of the day. In the interest in time, I will not explain each one – then I would be doing what my husband calls trying to fit 8 pounds of nails into a six-pound bag. But the spirit of each Law and the Spirit of the change that Jesus offers are all the same. Jesus' teachings are all about going ***above and beyond*** the Law. Each law deals with what a follower of Yahweh is PERMITTED to do in the name of justice and within the cultural norms of Moses' day. Jesus reminds us that we CAN do those things, or we can CHOOSE a different approach. We can give up our right to retaliate. We can give up love with limits.

The second basic discipleship commitment that Jesus offers has to do with how we should treat our enemies. Jesus again begins, "You have heard that it was said, 'You shall love your neighbor'' quoting the Law from Leviticus. When given in its original intent, this law focused on WHO your neighbor is. But the "Hate your enemy part" is more of a summation of several parts of the Law. It is never plainly stated in Old Testament Scripture. So when the crowd who was listening heard this, they would have thought, "Well, I will love my next-door neighbor but not those filthy Samaritans or unclean Gentiles. It is expected for me to hate those who have been our enemies for hundreds of years."

Jesus once again teaches that we must go above and beyond the Law. He adds: "But I say to you, love your enemies and pray for those who persecute you." This does not focus on our relationship with God as much as it does on being a person who shares the characteristics that God displays to us with other people. We are to give up loving with limits and show others what it looks like to share God's love with everyone. And Jesus doesn't simply suggest that we should love others or praise us for loving others. Jesus commands it.

It is important to realize that Jesus is not talking about brotherly love or affectionate love. Jesus is talking about ***agape*** love. This love requires us to be concerned about the welfare of others. This means that we will do things that benefit them. It does not say that if someone has done something horrendous to you – if you have been molested or abused or publicly slandered – that you are to ***like*** them. You do not have to play golf with them or invite them to lunch. But you are to pray for their well-being, their health and their security.

Jesus DOES mean that when we give up love with limits, when we become disciples of Christ, we forgo the right to give people what they deserve, to seek revenge or exact retaliation. Instead we can CHOOSE to live like Jesus and go above and beyond the Law. So we are to love and pray for those we like and those we don't like. Just as God does not send rain only to those who deserve it.

Of course, we all know that this is easier said than done. In truth, I am sure that everyone here wishes that they ***could*** love without limits. But we live in a fallen world, full of unlovable people who do unlovable things. So it might be helpful to remember one of my favorite C. S. Lewis quotes: "Do not waste time bothering whether you love your neighbor; act as if you did. As soon as we do this, we find one of the great secrets.

When you are behaving as if you loved someone you will presently come to love him." Or to put it into modern day vernacular – fake it 'til you make it!

I am sure we can all recall times when we have made the choice to treat someone in a way that was not in line with how we have been treated. And we can recall how unnatural it was, how it went against our basic instincts. Here is a case in point from my own life.

Last year, we participated in writing a series of Lenten Devotions with several other Presbyterian Churches in Spartanburg County. You may remember that many of us wrote about people that were ordinary heroes to us. I wrote about my mother-in-law, Marilynn, who lived this command from Jesus better than anyone I have ever known.

When I was in my early thirties, I went through a very difficult situation. During that time, some people who I thought were my friends, good "church going" people who had taught me how to live, disagreed with me in a very public and hurtful way. I was so disheartened because they did not live in the way that they had taught me. They talked the talk but did not walk the walk. And in their treatment of me, they actually ended up persecuting me for seeking righteousness.

There were many days when I wanted to retaliate, to treat them the way that I was being treated. And I would turn to Marilynn to vent my anger and disillusionment. Every time, she would listen sympathetically, agree that I was being treated horribly and then offer the same words 'Just smother them with kindness and they'll come around." Friends, this is basically a summary of the second discipleship commitment that Jesus is seeking in these words from the Sermon on the Mount. Because when you kill your enemies with kindness you are giving up love with limits. You are loving the way that Jesus commands. And you are being more like God.

And by the way when I tried her advice – it worked! I was kind, even when it killed me. And the situation ultimately resolved itself. Of course, our natural tendency is to strike out with unkind words. Repay as we have BEEN paid. But even to this day, I have found when I follow her advice, people have no choice but to return my kindness after a while. Of course, a lot of prayer and work of the Holy Spirit goes into bringing about reconciliation, but it all begins with the seed of kindness planted along with the sincere hope of a resolution. It requires giving up love with limits.

So as we continue to observe a Holy Lent, a time of spiritual discernment that will help us grow more like our Savior each day, his words call us to give up our rights and die to self. Living only for God and for God's kingdom. And to smother those who hurt us with kindness, showing them the grace that God shares with us each day. It is easy to focus on Jesus' person and work as our only example of perfection, but when we chose to give up love with limits, we are closer to becoming perfect as our Heavenly Father is perfect. In the name of the Father and of the Son and of the Holy Spirit. Amen.

More than Chocolate: Giving up Fear

Isaiah 43:1; Mark 4:35-41

Many of you have heard me speak of my Lenten practice of drawing the name of a person out of a bag each morning and praying very intentionally for them all day long. I usually text the person first thing and ask if they have any special requests. One day this week, I drew the name of a fellow pastor and her reply really gave me a lump in my throat. I won't mention her name because the prayer requests are confidential, but this is what she asked: "Please pray for my ability to share with parents of our youth the questions their young people asked last night about the state of our world and their fears and desires to stop violence and prejudice."

What thoughtful young people she must have in her church. And I think they articulated the fears that many of us have. Fear is prevalent in our individual lives, and in our corporate lives in the communities, schools, and even churches in which we live and work. And if the state of the world is not enough to scare us, there are plenty of other things that bring anxiety to our lives. Fear of disapproval, rejection, failure, illness, losing one's jobs, money problems, isolation, aging – the list could go on and on.

And so we might stop and wonder if being in a boat on a lake in the middle of a storm is worthy of the terror that the disciples exhibited but let's take a closer look at their circumstances. Jesus is with his disciples in a boat on the Sea of Galilee. Mark tells us earlier in the chapter that so many people had started to follow them that he got into the boat, went out into the lake and preached there. All day, his pulpit had been the very boat. Finally, at the end of the day, exhausted from preaching and teaching and sharing parables with everyone, Jesus told the disciples to move away from the shore and fell into a much-needed sleep.

But as it often happened on the Sea of Galilee, a great storm came up out of nowhere. The Greek word used is actually "whirlwind", conjuring up all sorts of pictures of violence and turbulence in my mind. I can all but see the winds causing the lake to foam all around them, jumping up high like angry monsters waving their whitecapped fists. And what started out as a simple time of rest, away from the growing crowds, became an evening of fear and tumultuous emotions as the terrified disciples woke Jesus up and said, "Don't you care what is happening?"

As modern Christians who know that Jesus proceeded to calm the seas with his voice, it is sometimes easy to criticize the disciples and wonder, like Jesus did, why they don't have more faith. But let's look at it this way - basically what you have is a community of believers in Jesus Christ, who, in the guise of disciples, are challenged to trust Jesus more. And when their faith in his presence was really tested, they cried out, "Don't you care?" Sound like anyone you know?

Well, it should. Because everyone here has been in such a storm, EVEN if you've NEVER been in a boat! You are rowing along, headed for the finish line when all of the sudden, out of the blue - the test comes back positive. Your daughter gets divorced. The car won't start, the baby is sick, you drop your cell phone in the bathtub, or there is a traffic jam on the interstate.

Whether it is a disaster of great proportions or a seemingly insignificant bump in the road, an unexpected storm will bring to us the SAME emotions that the disciples experienced in the boat. Fear, terror, feelings of abandonment. The good news is that the reaction of Jesus can calm OUR storms the same way he did the storm on the Sea of Galilee as we seek to give up fear.

You see, this story helps us answer questions that will strengthen our faith. And when you get right down to it, faith is the opposite of fear. The question that the disciples ask is this: Who is this Jesus? They are seeing firsthand that Jesus has command over the created world. By calming the storm, Jesus does something that is normally reserved for God. This is so startling that it causes the disciples to pose the question, "Who is this that even the wind and the sea obey him?" And in the Gospel of Mark, where Jesus seems so intent on keeping his identity a secret, it is an important step in setting his closest friends on the path to discovery.

But that is not the same question that we have, because we already know that Jesus was present at the creation of the world. It stands to reason that he has dominion over that which he made. So in our quest to give up fear, a more important question is "Who is Jesus ***in my life***"? Does Jesus have authority over the chaos that you and I face? Do we seek his wisdom through prayer and Scripture and truly being modern day disciples who are surrounded daily by those with like minds?

And if we can answer "yes" truthfully to all of those questions, then why ***would*** we fear? Well, maybe it is because this story sheds light on the Divine side of Jesus, and we need to have the human side, the "God walking around with skin on" Jesus when we are afraid.

Minster Reynolds Price tells of an 87-year-old woman who wrote to him about one of those moments when she needed the human Jesus in her life. She was facing a time of difficulty as she was going through exhausting medical tests in preparation for surgery. One day she had a kind of vision. "I went out along the Galilee hills and came to a crowd gathered around a man, and I stood on the outskirts intending to listen. In my vision, I could see that the man is God. But he looked over the crowd at me and then said, 'What do you want?' And I said, 'Could you send someone to come with me and help me stand up after the tests because I can't manage alone?' The man thought for a moment and then said, 'How would it be if I came?'" (1)

This is so relevant because when you think of it, Jesus does not say that there is nothing to fear. He simply says, "DO NOT BE AFRAID". Jesus knows that we live in a fearful world full of fallen people who will do terrible things. In fact, it is probably wise to have a certain amount of fear. No, Jesus says that fear does not have the last word when we confront it with God by our side.

This is precisely what God has done in Jesus Christ. Jesus is Emmanuel, God with us. God has come to us in our suffering and pain, in our struggle to be human, in our fear and anxiety, and in our doubt and uncertainty. Jesus put off deity and put on humanity. He became one of us--one with us--one for us. That is why the prophet Isaiah shares the promise of God, "Do not fear, I have redeemed you. I have called you by name, you are mine." When we belong to God, when we know that God walks with us in every storm in life, we can give up fear.

But perhaps an even more important question for Jesus' disciples then and now is this: "Have you invited Jesus to come into the storms in your life?" The disciples did. They said, "Wake up - don't you care what is happening?" Yet even after they invited him in, they were a little hesitant to allow him to ride out the storm with them. Their invitation was somewhat half-hearted.

I say this because, after they witnessed the miracle of Jesus calming the storm, Mark tells us that the disciples were filled with great awe. But the word "awe" in Greek can also be translated as "fear". This means that, even when they began to suspect that Jesus was God himself, they were still afraid. The idea that God was with them so closely scared them almost as much as God not being with them.

And maybe it is because real miracles upset people! We see this throughout Scripture in the Pharisees reactions to Jesus' healing or when the townspeople were so afraid after witnessing a miracle that they begged Jesus to leave their neighborhood. (Matthew 8:34) You can bet there were some folks who were upset when Lazarus climbed up out of the tomb after four days of being dead because it is not what we expect. Miracles force us all to come face-to-face with the power of God, the mystery of God, and we all know that we tend to fear anything that we cannot explain.

One of my favorite ministers and story tellers is Fred Craddock. He tells the about a pastor he knew who went to visit one of his parishioners in the hospital. The woman was suffering from a terminal disease, and the pastor went to visit her knowing that, at the end of that visit, he would pray one of those prayers that acknowledges the desperation of the situation. A prayer that puts it out there on the table that not much is going to change. A prayer to help the woman and her family move towards acceptance.

As a minister, I knew what kind of prayer he was speaking of, as I have prayed them often. They are honest and pastorally sensitive, and often they are the only appropriate kinds of prayers to pray. They go something like this. "Oh God, we thank you that you are with us in every circumstance, even this one. And so we simply ask that you give us the courage to accept your will for our future, whatever that will is. Now we place ourselves, with trust, in your all-knowing hands."

The pastor went there prepared to pray that kind of prayer, as Craddock tells the story. But the woman prevailed upon him to beg God to heal her. And so, against his better judgment, he prayed a different kind of prayer altogether. He prayed fervently, even while he understood what a long shot that prayer was. And then when that prayer was over, he left that room.

But a few days later he was back for another visit. The woman was sitting up in the bed. The tubes had been removed, and the curtains were open. She said to him, "You won't believe what has happened. The doctors noticed some changes the other day, and called for more x-rays, and they have told me that they can no longer see any sign of a tumor! I'm going home tomorrow." The pastor said later, "When I got out to the parking lot, I looked up into the skies and said, 'Don't ever do that to me again!'"

Friends, it was fear of the unexplainable, the mystery surrounding Jesus that led to his death on the cross. But we know that his death, which seemed like the worst day in the history of humanity, proved to be the greatest gift for all people and for all time because it is God's gift of Eternal life to each one here. So rather than choosing to live in fear because it is what we are used to, because it is understandable, even predictable, this story in the boat begs us to invite Jesus into the storms of life so that God can turn our fear into grace.

There is a contemporary Christian song that explains what I am trying to say better than I can. Listen to some of the words. "Sometimes He calms the storm with a whispered 'Peace, be still'. He can settle any sea, but it doesn't mean He will. Sometimes He holds us close and lets the wind and waves go wild. Sometimes He calms the storm. Other times He calms His child."

Friends, the prevailing thought in this story is that no matter what kind of fears we are faced with, when we know who Jesus is in our lives and invite him to enter into our storms, that God will either calm the storm or calm our fears. He has called us each by name and we are His. In the name of the Father and of the Son and of the Holy Spirit. Amen.

(1) Reynolds Price, *Letter to a Man in a Fire*, Simon & Schuster, NY, NY, 1999, 30-31

More Than Chocolate: Giving up Our Wills

Ephesians 4:17-24; Mark 8:27-35

When we visited the Holy Land, it seemed like every day we went somewhere named Caesarea. This is because so many places were built to honor Caesar Augustus. At Caesarea Maritime, we saw the remains of the palace built on the Mediterranean where Caesar spent his summers. This included the room where Paul was interrogated before he was sent to Rome for his last trial and possible death. Today's story takes place in Caesarea Philippi, made into the capital by Philip – son of Herold the Great and hence the name. As you can see, the Caesars had big egos!

Mark says that Jesus and his disciples are travelling in the villages around Caesarea Philippi which means that they were almost half-way between Galilee and Jerusalem. Jesus' ministry in Galilee is finished and they are turning toward Jerusalem. Of course, at this point Jesus knows he is headed toward the cross. So he and his disciples are both physically and symbolically between two places where they cannot only look forward and but also look back.

Having been in the region, I think it is significant to note that the disciples would also have been surrounded by so many physical reminders of other gods in this place. The temple built to honor Caesar, representing the government. Idols built to honor Zeus, the Greek god of all gods and the king of sky and thunder as well as one built to honor Pan, the god of shepherds and nature.

It is in the midst of these surroundings and based on where they have been and where they are headed, that Jesus asks the disciples, "Who do people say that I am?" He receives a variety of answers. Then he asks a more important question. "Who do YOU say that I am?"

He asks them this question because who ***Jesus*** is and what ***he*** does are intimately related to who his ***disciples*** are and what will be required of them. Peter answers immediately, in true Peter fashion, "YOU ARE THE MESSIAH!"

The truth is that this was a really bold answer for Peter. During the 400 years in between the prophet Malachi's promise that a Messiah was coming and the preaching of John the Baptist, some very definite ideas had developed among the Jews as to what the Messiah would look like. The common belief was that a time of terrible tribulation would prevail on earth. Then, when things were as bad as they could get, Elijah would enter history again as a forerunner to the Christ and the Messiah would appear.

Once he arrived, all the nations would come together and there would be total destruction of the powers in the world that were hostile to the children of Yahweh. Jerusalem would be renovated and the Jews that had been dispersed all over the land would be gathered back to Palestine, which would be the center of the world. And from then on, peace and goodness would reign forever.

This is a radically different picture from the world that the Jews of Jesus' day were living in. Governed by Rome and living daily with oppression, they begin to hear that the Son of God has finally come! But instead of being a warrior who would prevail against the enemy, he is an ordinary man who travels with twelve questionable characters and eats with sinners, talks to women in the streets and heals on the Sabbath. It is no wonder so few people recognized Jesus for who he was.

Nevertheless, after Peter confirms his Lordship, Jesus then tells them where they are headed. Towards Jerusalem, where he will suffer and die and rise again and where they will be asked to take up his cross and follow him. And in keeping with our Lenten Sermon Series, "More Than Chocolate", I think Jesus is telling all disciples in every time and place that when we pledge to take up the cross and follow him, we will be giving up our will. In other words, when we make the claim that Peter did and say that Jesus is the Son of God, the Savior, then we will be following HIS will and not our own.

Now I don't know exactly what it meant for someone in first Century Palestine to deny themselves, but for 21st century American Christians, it is a pretty radical step! In our Western way of thinking, the predominant idea is that everyone has a "right" to do what they want. We often think that we can pursue happiness at all costs. We hear the mantra, "If it feels good, do it!" We tell our children and grandchildren they can be anything they want when they grow up. I agree with the importance of building a positive self-image in our children and ourselves, but I can't help but wonder if we haven't taken the whole concept a bit too far.

You see, what Jesus is saying is that to be his follower means that we must say NO to the self that wants to seek comfort, status and personal gain. We must make plans, use our gifts and work towards building up the kingdom of God and God's will rather than seeking our desires. And this is hard for many modern-day Americans because we live in a FedEx, drive-through, Instagram world where we get what we want, when we want it, according to our ***own*** will.

As I wrote this, I remembered the time when our daughter Katie was 6 and declared one day that she was going to become a vegetarian. Her resolved lasted until the next day when we went to McDonald's and I asked if she wanted a salad. When she said, "No – I want a Happy Meal" I reminded her of new healthy endeavors and she quickly decided that she had denied herself of cheeseburgers for long enough.

Now to her credit, the first part of giving up our will – TO DENY OURSELVES – is tough for anyone. So it helps me to remember that Jesus never calls us to do ANYTHING that he himself has not already done. The story is told of a famous Roman general who was discussing with this staff how to take a difficult position. Someone suggested a certain course of action and remarked, "It will only cost the lives of a few". The general immediately responded by asking, "Are YOU willing to be one of the few?" Jesus was not the kind of leader who sat remotely and played with the lives of his followers like expendable pawns. What he demanded THEY should face, he too, was ready to face. This strengthens our belief that Jesus has the right to call us to give up our will and deny ourselves because he has already done so and will do it with us.

The same is true in the next part of Jesus' command to Peter which also calls us to give up our will. "TAKE UP YOUR CROSS", Jesus says. Jesus knows the burden and pain, the sheer weight of the cross he would struggle to carry up the hill of Calvary. While we were in Jerusalem, we walked what is known as the Via Dolorosa, of the "Way of Suffering" – the path from the courtroom where Jesus was convicted to the hill where he was crucified.

Three places along the way, there are signs to note that Jesus stumbled in that spot. One sign marks the place where a man named Simon of Cyrene was asked to help Jesus with his task. It reminded me that, while none of us knows what it means to physically carry that cross, there are ways that we can carry the cross when we understand the burden that someone else is carrying and choose to minister to them.

If you have lost a child, you KNOW the pain that no one else can truly understand and can share your heart with that person who must bury a son. If you have lost your health, you can empathize with the one who may only see hopelessness and assure them that God will give them the strength to find a way of coping with new circumstances. If you have been abused, or punished for speaking the truth, or lost a spouse or faced ANY hardship then you can carry the cross for someone else who is shouldering the same burden by simply being an empathetic listener or by supporting them with your prayers and friendship.

And I believe that when we give up our will by denying ourselves and picking up the cross, then and ONLY then will we be able to follow Jesus' third part of his command to Peter. This is the same invitation that he made to the fishermen who left their employment to join his band of disciples. It is the invitation that he made throughout his whole ministry and makes even today. FOLLOW ME. But this call has been redefined for us because today, we see that invitation with the cross in mind and understand that to follow Jesus will ultimately lead only to glory.

The last line of our Scripture this morning could easily be regarded as a proverb of Jesus because he said it so often. One might even say that it is a summary of what Jesus calls us to do when we give up our will. But William Barclay's interpretation on this line gives it an even more positive spin. He says that Jesus means that certain things are lost when saved and other things are saved by being lost. What a twist! When we give up our will, we are actually gaining rather than losing because we are living within the will of God.

Isn't that a wonderful message and a perfect way to think about denying ourselves, picking up the cross and following Jesus? Let's explore it a little deeper. What THINGS has God given you? The ability to teach, to sing, to knit. A beautiful smile or an infectious laugh. The gift of knowing when to be silent. The gift of being able to encourage or perhaps of simply being present. Then consider this - are you losing these things because you are saving them? Or are you saving them because they are being used?

In a way, that is what Paul offers us in his letter to the Ephesians. He reminds us that when we give up our will, when we put on the new life in Christ, we don't so much give up something as we do receive something more. When we clothe our will with the new self, created in the likeness of God and according to GOD's WILL and righteousness, we are sharing the gift of salvation by the sharing the gifts that God brings to our lives in Jesus Christ.

And just this morning, we were all privileged to witness this call to give up our will in one of the most beautiful and meaningful sacraments of our faith. Baptism. Today, when Katie and Benjamin decided to bring their son to the baptismal font, they were pledging to help Robert give up his will and seek God's will for the rest of his life. And we all did the same. When we answered "we do" to the question posed to us to help guide Robert in the ways of the Lord, we were promising to show him what our new lives in Christ are clothed with.

And as those who are called to put on the new clothing of Christ by being baptized into his life, death and resurrection, we are also called to ask ourselves today and every day if we are willing to follow the commandment that Jesus gave Peter. And in giving up our will, we are acknowledging the hope that we have when we say to him, "You are the Christ in my life and so I want to follow YOUR will". This is a hope that will enable us by God's grace and love to deny ourselves, follow him and stand at the foot of the cross which is now planted on the hill of our salvation. In the name of the Father and of the Son and of the Holy Spirit. Amen.

More than Chocolate: Giving up the Need for Approval

John 12:12-19

Do you remember around the year 2005 when the flash mob became popular? It was sometimes described as a random act of culture. A flash mob usually started with two or three people in a crowded public place who would begin a seemingly pointless performance. They would soon be joined by more and more people until the song or act was finished and then quickly disperse. Flash mobs often took place in malls, in large downtown squares or other places where large crowds were gathered.

I watched several You Tube videos of popular flash mobs when I started preparing this sermon and it seems that the most-used songs were Michael Jackson's "Beat It" and "The Hallelujah Chorus!" An odd statement on our society. They took place all over the world and, somehow or another, always left me, and I assume the real observers, with a smile and an overall good feeling.

Well a flash mob is what I immediately thought of when I started reading the background on who was present the day that Jesus entered Jerusalem on what we now call Pam Sunday. As I read about how the people assembled there, I could almost hear a rock song playing in the background and see the palms waving to the beat.

According to John, the first people to follow Jesus in were the ones who were present when Jesus raised Lazarus from the dead. Jesus was in the nearby village of Bethany and when the people saw that he brought Mary and Martha's beloved brother back to life, many of them joined the band of believers who recognized that he was the Messiah and followed him to Jerusalem, only two miles away. So in our culture, they would have been the instigators of the flash mob.

As they entered Jerusalem, they would have encountered a TRUE mob of people who had come to the Temple to celebrate the Passover. This was one of the three compulsory festivals for Jews and those followers of Yahweh who had been dispersed throughout the land in previous years often came to Jerusalem to worship and make sacrifices to their God. Estimates of how many people came were made by the number of lambs that were sold for slaughter. The historian Josephus writes that one lamb was needed per ten people when they entered the Temple.

Using this fact as a calculator, there were most likely 2.7 million extra Jews in Jerusalem when Jesus and his band arrived a few days before the Passover feast took place. Of course, rumors of his raising Lazarus were spreading like wildfire, so a third group of people may have joined up with the crowd simply out of curiosity.

But what caused them to hail him as a King? Was it the news that he had brought a dead man to life? Was it the other miracles that they had heard about? Did the disciples ***ask*** them to gather and pay him homage? Or was is a combination of all these things? The most likely answer is that people just got caught up in the moment, in doing what everyone else was doing. And as I prepared for this sermon in our Lenten Series,

"Giving up Chocolate", I realized that Jesus' actions and the REACTIONS of the people could be seen as a comment on giving up the need for approval.

Let's look at the people first. The crowd gathered on that first Palm Sunday behaved just like a flash mob. When one small group started to hail Jesus as King, throwing their cloaks on the ground for the donkey to walk on and waving their Palm Branches in the air, the others followed suit. Hosanna literally means "Hooray for salvation! It's coming! It's here!" Listening to the flash mob, we would say that Jesus' approval rating was quite high on that day.

However, as people came to learn that Jesus would not become their King the way they had hoped, many of them would no longer be shouting words of praise. Instead, in just five days, some of these same people would be shouting words of death, "Crucify Him! Crucify Him!" How could that be? What happened to change their minds so quickly? What did Jesus do to cause such a drastic drop in His approval rating?

The truth is that the people who hailed Jesus that day had no real sense of commitment. They just went along with the crowd. They chose what was popular without even thinking about what was right. I think we develop this mentality early in life, wanting to fit in at the sandbox or to be invited to sit at the popular girls table. And it takes real integrity and a few hard lessons learned to stand up for what we believe, when we know it is right, even when our friends do not agree.

Several years ago, my husband and I went to New Orleans to a National YMCA Convention when he was serving on the

Greenville Metro YMCA Board. We were privileged to hear Baptist Minister and sociologist Tony Campolo speak. He told a story I will never forget. When Tony was in college in the late 1950's, he admitted that he joined in with a crowd of friends who bullied a young man that was a homosexual in their class. He said that, even as they all did things that were cruel, that he was ashamed of, he participated in the activities anyway because he was afraid that, if he did not, his friends would think ***he*** was gay or even just sympathetic to gays. Of course, in the 50's this would have been completely socially unacceptable.

When we heard him speak, he remarked that, no matter how he felt about someone who was gay, he knew that as a person who professed to be a Christian, what he was doing was wrong. But his convictions were not strong enough to keep him from participating or stop his friends from doing that which he knew was unjust. That day, he even teared up a little and said that he wished he knew what had become of the young man, so he could find him and apologize.

I thought it was admirable and very brave of him tell this story, not knowing how we would receive his confession. But his faith had deepened enough that he knew it was more important to speak up about injustice, even if it would not be popular with the crowd.

It is easy to see how detrimental peer pressure can be to our young people who must face choices that most of us who are thirty and older did not have to face when we were growing up. It is horrifying to read and hear about children being faced with drugs and gang violence in elementary and middle schools. But reading the story of Jesus' entry into Jerusalem and knowing how easily the crowd would change their allegiance is a reminder that peer pressure never really stops plaguing us. It is only when we give up the need for approval that we can stand strong in our convictions when they are not what others around us believe in. The crowd in Jerusalem did not understand this.

But there is another group in this story that should not be ignored either as we think about giving up the need for approval. They are the reason I chose John's version of Jesus' triumphal entry into Jerusalem over the other gospel writers. Only John includes the statement of the Pharisees: "You see, you can do nothing. Look, the world has gone after him."

Even as wrong as they were, the Pharisees did not stick to what they really believed was right. They did not stop pursuing Jesus in that moment because they suddenly realized that he truly ***was*** the Messiah. They simply threw their hands up in the air and basically said, "We will never win the war when this many people are against us." They, too, sought the approval of those around them at the time. It was easier to stand in the crowd and do nothing than to stand up for what they thought was right.

Of course, the flip side of the coin, the one that we all want to emulate – no matter our age, our maturity level or place on the path of spiritual wisdom – is Jesus Christ. Jesus did not care about approval ratings. He made a very deliberate statement when he rode into town on a donkey. You see, although he was fulfilling the prophecy of Zechariah, who 500 years before Jesus was born predicted that the Messiah would ride into town on a donkey's colt, he also knew that what people WANTED, what they EXPECTED, what they thought they NEEDED was a soldier, a king who would go to battle with weapons.

The children of Israel had been oppressed for hundreds of years. They had lived through slavery in Egypt, escaped to wander the desert for many years, basically homeless, and then fought many pagan peoples to retain the privilege of living in the Promised Land that God had said belonged to them. They had been conquered by the Assyrians, exiled to Babylon and finally come home only to live under Roman oppression.

So, it is understandable that the Jews wanted a king who would come with sword and might and passion and put the Emperor in his place and reclaim the land and power that was rightfully theirs. And while in first Century Palestine a donkey was considered a noble animal, a king bent on war would come riding into town on a horse. Everyone knew this!

Jesus knew it too. He knew what the people wanted of him. He knew the statement that they were looking for. Yet, he CHOSE to come riding into town on a donkey, which translated to everyone that he was a King who was bent on peace. He would use the weapons of justice, faith and righteousness, which is something that few can really understand, even today. People were looking for the Messiah of their dreams and Jesus came as the Messiah whom God had sent.

So, while the people drifted from one side of the aisle to the other, as easily as the wind blows, shouting "SALVATION IS HERE" one day, and "CRUCIFY HIM" the next, Jesus did

NOT change. He did not seek approval and popularity and political gain. He sought ONLY the approval of his Father.

Only Jesus stays the course in this story. Jesus came into Jerusalem with the specific purpose of going to Calvary for our salvation. He came to do the Father's will and he would let nothing stop him from doing what he knew needed to be done. He would not let the Roman government stop him. He would not let the religious leaders stop Him. He would not let the applause of the people stop him. Jesus didn't care what humankind thought. He only cared about what His Heavenly Father thought.

When I told my husband what we were giving up today, he laughed and asked if I was going to look in the mirror and preach this sermon to myself. And truth be told ALL of us need affection and approval, but some of us more than others. I fall into that category. I am a terrible people pleaser and have to daily struggle to let the Holy Spirit lead me to do the right thing, the courageous thing, the noble thing. And friends, I often fail! It is so much easier to preach what people want to hear than it is preach, as John the Baptist did, "Repent, you sinners. The kingdom of God is at hand!"

So it is my prayer as we walk through this Holy Week in whatever ways we can, that we will all continue to work, worship, study, play and live to the best of our ability and to do it all for the glory of God. Let us not do it for the applause of man, but rather, for the applause of God. It's been said, "Leaders act on conviction, performers act on applause." Jesus wasn't some Hollywood Oscar nominee acting for the applause of man. His applause would come later as He ascended to heaven. May it be the same for you and me. May we seek to be spiritual leaders, following the will of God and not earthly followers who simply join up with the flash mob and dance to the song of the moment. May we dance to the glory of God and to the Christ who saves us all. In the name of the Father and of the Son and of the Holy Spirit. Amen.

More Than Chocolate: Giving up Superiority

John 13:1-15

When I am asked what my favorite Gospel is, my answer is always hands down – the Gospel of John. Many call it a spiritual biography because it is so different from the other three – the Synoptic Gospels, as they are called. In John we have no manger, no baptism of Jesus, no institution of the Last Supper. There are no miracles in John. Instead John writes about "signs" – all performed to convince the people present that Jesus truly is God. One of those signs is Jesus raising Lazarus from the dead.

Right before Jesus called Lazarus back to life, he said to the crowd that had followed him to the tomb, "Did I not tell you that if you believed, you would see the glory of God?" Then he said to God, so that everyone present could hear him, "I have said this for the sake of the crowd standing here, so that they may believe that you sent me." If you were in church Sunday, you know that Jesus' technique worked, and many followed him into Jerusalem, shouting, "Hosanna! Salvation is here!"

Yet even though they believed, they did not understand. They believed Jesus was God, but they still did not understand that he would be different from the God of their ancestors. They believed that he would save them but did not understand it would be in a different way. Let me explain.

The Jews who stood by Mary and Martha as their dead brother emerged from the tomb thought that God was going to deliver them once more. The God of the Exodus had seen their misery, heard their cries, and entered into their affliction. He showed them love by delivering them out of slavery and into the Promised Land. So when Jesus displayed such a godly characteristic as raising someone from the dead, they assumed he would deliver them in the same way. That he would show power they way that God had before – through plagues and angels of death and parting of seas and the crushing of armies.

Imagine the utter confusion and even horror of the disciples when, after they had celebrated the Passover, rather than acting like the superior king, the consummate leader, the powerful God who would show triumphant love, he instead took the form of a servant. This was a completely different kind of love. This was a love of service. Instead of delivering them from the power of death, he was offering himself. Completely. Freely. He was giving up superiority.

You see, THIS King of the Jews had a completely different understanding of power. Jesus demonstrated with his actions and then followed up with his words that to truly be great, for any of us to have REAL power, we must be willing to give up superiority and become humble servants.

This was true from the beginning of his life. God could have come to earth and lived in a palace or The Temple. He could have been welcomed by learned rabbis or governors or princes. He could have been born to people of wealth and lived in a house carved out of sandstone or marble. He could have even come as a fully-grown king who rode into town on a white steed with a powerful army behind him. But God came to us as a baby instead. He came to earth as one who was so vulnerable and completely dependent on others and then began his journey as the suffering servant.

So tonight, we come to celebrate the humility that Jesus lived with, served with and died with because he chose to give up superiority. Author Susan Lenzkes writes: "Jesus left the Hallowed halls of heaven which were lined with jewels and landed cold, wet and squirming on a pile of straw." And that is what we are called to emulate as we continue our Lenten Series – "More than Chocolate". We are called to give up superiority. In fact, tonight we not only give it, but we celebrate doing so.

In the Reformed tradition, you know that we only have two sacraments. They are baptism and the Lord's Supper. Sacraments are visible symbols of the reality of God that are considered holy ways to enact God's grace. By that definition, baptism and the Lord's Supper are sacraments because they are tangible pictures of our forgiveness through Christ that help us remember God's supernatural saving faith. Baptism displays the washing away of sins through the Holy Spirit. The Lord's Supper is a powerful reminder that Jesus gave his blood and body on the cross so that all who are forgiven could enjoy fellowship with him in his Father's kingdom.

But if we are to take Jesus' last act of love in John's gospel before his crucifixion to be true instruction for each one here, then perhaps we should reconsider our traditions. Because if Jesus could make changes to our modern-day worship, he might suggest a third sacrament. And I will be so bold as to say that if we were to have a third sacrament, it would be servanthood.

John begins this story by reminding us of Jesus' authority. Jesus knew that the Father had given all things into his hands. He reminds us of his Divine origin by calling us "his own" and Jesus reminds us that he knew where he was going – back to His Father. Any of ***us*** who truly understood such power and might and future glory would most likely be too puffed up with pride and dignity to think of anything other than our own greatness.

But not Jesus Christ. He is a **God** of greatness but a **man** of humility. And so, knowing all this about himself, he chose to share this last meal with his disciples and to wash their feet. Jesus was a true servant. And a true servant of God does not minister for personal gain; he ministers to help others grow in the faith. His actions were for them – for their growth and spiritual maturity. Jesus wanted to be sure that his closest friends understood that his entire ministry was one of love and service and giving up superiority so that others could understand what it means to become followers of God.

John writes: "And during supper Jesus, knowing that the Father had given all things into his hands, got up from the table, took off his outer robe, and tied a towel around himself. Then he poured water into a basin and began to wash the disciples' feet and to wipe them with the towel that was tied around him." One of the commentaries that I used called this story a parable – that is a story with double meaning. I thought this was curious, so I began to examine the story more closely.

John tells us that Jesus got up – that is to say he bodily rose from the table. We can say that this action parallels Jesus' willingness to rise up from the throne of glory when he came into the world. He certainly could have remained where he was – comfortable in his creator status in Heaven. But Jesus loves you and me enough to give up comfort for inconvenience if it meant that He could show us how to abide in His Father's will.

Then Jesus took off his outer robe. But he had already done this when he laid aside his glory and became a man. When God came to earth, he could have done it JUST as the divine. He could have remained in his superior status. But because he is a God of grace, he wanted to experience personhood. So, he ruled by showing us that he was willing to experience disappointment, grief, friendship, betrayal, confusion, joy, family relationships – even hunger and thirst – on our behalf. The divine mixed with the human and for thirty-three years and Jesus felt everything you and I would ever have to experience by dealing with the mire and muck of our world.

The parable continues when John tells us that Jesus tied a towel around himself. A towel – the simple garment of a servant. God himself chose to assume a position of servanthood that the disciples could relate to because they had been known to argue among themselves as to who was the greatest. Richard Foster in his book *Celebration of Discipline* says that no one wanted to be considered the least. Then Jesus took a towel and a basin and so redefined greatness. And rather than STAND on his greatness, Jesus chose to KNEEL at the feet of his brethren, in a position of complete servitude.

But the final act of the parable is the one that we celebrate tonight as we come to the table and eat the meal that Jesus prepared for us that night long ago. John tells us that Jesus poured water into a basin. This can only symbolize the blood that Jesus would soon sacrifice for the atonement of our sins. God knew that the only substitute for human SIN was human BLOOD, so he offered his son in the place of you and me. The bread that we break together reminds us of the physical suffering on our behalf that Jesus endured. The cup reminds us that every drop of blood that flowed from the hands and feet of the crucified savior represents another one of our sins that has been forgiven.

The moral of the parable comes when Jesus asks the disciples, "Do you know what I have done? I have set you an example that you also should do as I have done to you." The lesson of the parable is that we are all called to take a servant role in God's kingdom. Indeed, this is how we give up superiority and reenact the last parable of Jesus in our own lives. In this way, servanthood becomes the third sacrament.

Many of the parables of Jesus are hard to understand but not this one. We can understand it because we begin in the same place that Jesus began in. In participating in God's call to service, we understand that giving up superiority means that we are to care for those who can no longer care for themselves; to get close to those who are suffering and alleviate their suffering; to open our homes, our hearts and our arms to the lonely; to honor others before we honor ourselves. Because when we yield to Christ and serve others, only then can we enter into the fullness of life that God has prepared for each one here. (1)

And in his final lesson to us, it is significant to note that Jesus served the meal to ***all*** those present, even Judas Iscariot, who he knew would betray him. This part of the parable reminds us that we cannot pick and choose who we would serve but to look at everyone we meet as a child of God, created in His image.

In the days that would follow this meal, Jesus would go on to demonstrate how great that love is. He would look into the faces of those who mocked him, spit on him, beat him and nailed him to a tree and say, "Father, forgive them, for they know not what they do." He would feel so betrayed by his own father that he would cry, "Abba, Father, why have you forsaken me?" He would experience all this and more on our behalf, so that Easter Sunday morning could truly be a joyful celebration of God's triumph over sin and evil in the world.

So friends, let us give up superiority and come as humble servants to the table of love. Remember the words, the face, and the touch of Jesus, who called us to be family to one another. Let us all come as servants, no one better or worse than the one who sits next to us in the pew, enacting the parable that Jesus gave us that night. Knowing that we are all saved by the body of sacrifice and the blood of humility. And may the forgiving grace of God enfold you and uphold you as we wait for the day of resurrection that is yet to come. Amen.

(1) Warren Wiersbe Be Transformed, Chariot Victor Publishing, 1986, chapter one.

More than Chocolate: Giving up Death

John 14:1-7, 25-28; Matthew 28:1-10

For those of you who have not been here every Sunday during Lent, I have been preaching a series of sermons entitled "More Than Chocolate". Each week, the sermon focused on something that God calls us to give up in our lives. These are things that pertain to our spiritual and emotional health. It was my hope that these sermons would call us to consider the obstacles that many of us face that prevent us from living into the faith and the discipleship that God desires for all of his children.

During Lent, we talked about giving up control, preconceived notions, love with limits, fear, our wills, the need for approval, and finally we considered giving up superiority as we follow Christ's last command to love and serve one another as God loves and serves us.

So it seemed only logical to me that, on Easter morning, we would give up death! That is what today is about. Giving up the last obstacle to our wholeness as we fully embrace the stronghold of our faith.

It seems that the older we get, the more we sense that death is greedy, swallowing up everyone we love, sometimes without warning. In fact, the death of a loved one is hard at any age. But as those who believe that the resurrection is a real event, we can claim as our last act of Lent that we are giving up death. Or at least that we are living as those who have no fear of death, as those who know that death will not be our final word.

Matthew's account of the resurrection is unique because it is a reminder that, while death is indeed very natural, there is NOTHING natural about resurrection. He stresses this by reporting on the peculiar acts of nature that accompany his version of that first Easter morning. If our Scripture today was made into a movie, it might win an Oscar for Special Affects!

Now no one went to the tomb that morning expecting to find it empty. Mary and Mary Magdalene only went there because they had a mission on their minds. You see, Jesus' body was buried in haste to comply with the Jewish law that calls for burial to take place before the beginning of the Sabbath, or sundown on Friday. But the Palestinian custom was to wrap the body in bands of linen that enclosed dry spices around the body. And the women in Jesus' life, knowing that the men who buried him were concerned only with adhering to the law in general assumed that they would not have taken time for the details of burial by properly anointing the body. And that is why the women went there – to comfort their Lord, even in his death. So they certainly expected to find his body there.

Yet, not only was the heavy stone that blocked the entrance to the tomb mysteriously rolled away, but Jesus was nowhere to be found. And if that is not supernatural enough, Matthew adds the great earthquake that shakes the ground with violence. An 8.3 on the Richter Scale that would have had the pottery falling off the tables and women on the way back from the well spilling their jugs of water as they fell to the ground and sheep scurrying out of their pens as the rock walls around them crumbled.

Then there is the angel sent from Heaven. And not a serene angel with a harp and a golden halo, but one who is accompanied by lightning bolts and clothing that is reminiscent of the Transfiguration, white as snow. And when the angels shook the guards who had been left to watch over the tomb, they immediately became paralyzed, frozen in their tracks. Literally scared to make a move!

This description of the first Easter Sunday is actually in line with the core of Matthew's theology. Matthew wanted the children of Israel to understand that Jesus was the fulfillment of the Messianic promise that they had waited for since God called them to be his people. Matthew's Jesus is a royal Jesus, emphasizing his role as King. So, he portrays the resurrection, not simply as Jesus coming back to life but as God erupting into the world in a new and decisive manner. Heralded by symbolic imagery and signs, we are totally aware that something new, something completely paranormal has happened.

Yet at just the moment in the movie when you or I want to grab the hand of our date and cover our eyes, the angel says to the women, "Do not be afraid!" And friends, that is how we know that Easter morning means that we can give up death. Because this was not a message delivered by another human who is just trying to bring comfort. This is God's message to everyone here.

As a pastor, I have spent a lot of time around illness and death. Yet, even when I am holding the hand of someone who is sure in their beliefs, I do not have the right to tell them not to be afraid as they are dying. I can tell them that they are not alone or that their family will be okay if they are tired of fighting, or that I am praying for them, but it is not my place to tell them not to be afraid.

Doctors do not have that right either. Even if they are able to monitor the amount of pain someone feels or predict the time that it will take to die. Yet, in the realm of humanity, death is the final conclusion of every life, even the one most faithfully lived. So for any fellow human to tell someone not to fear death is completely unreasonable. It is simply not our place.

But Jesus does have the right. Jesus has experienced it and know that death will not be the victor. Jesus tried to tell his followers this before his death although many did not understand him. After Jesus had washed the disciples' feet in John's Gospel and is trying to say his farewells, the disciples start to display their fears. Our favorite disciple, Peter, in his classic way of communicating with hyperbole, pledges to lay down his life for Jesus. Jesus knows that it is time to give them the reassurance that they need, so he leaves us all with one of the most pastoral soliloquies in all of Scripture.

"Do not let your hearts be troubled. Believe in God, believe also in me. In my Father's house there are many dwelling places. If it were not so, would I have told you that I go to prepare a place for you? And if I go and prepare a place for you, I will come again and will take you to myself, so that where I am, there you may be also".

This is the assurance from Jesus himself that, although they are getting ready to enter a time of doubt, anxiety and uncertainty, they can hold on to the promise that everyone who believes can truly give up death. That there is nothing to fear. Because Jesus is there waiting for us.

Some people use this passage in ways that try to take away our need to grieve and that was not Jesus' intent. He didn't say "Do not let your hearts be troubled", so that we would think that life is going to be fair and easy and soft, so that we wouldn't be sad when someone we die loves. He gave these words as a ***pastor*** to assure the ones who were going to be left on this earth – the ones who had to deal with the cruelties of life and illness and persecution and addiction and poverty and depression and politics – that they can still live with hope.

Last year, my husband and I attended a memorial service for a friend of ours who died at the age of 61 from early onset Alzheimer's. The Hospice chaplain who assisted in his service read this passage, at the request of the family, because it is one that always brings us comfort. John tells us that when Jesus promises the disciples that they will one day be with him, that good old doubting Thomas says, "Well, that's not very helpful – we don't even know where you are going", Jesus offers the words that are the bedrock of our faith.

Jesus said to him, "I am the way, and the truth, and the life. No one comes to the Father except through me." When we lose someone we love, we want to hear this promise that we can give up death. That we will live in eternity with him. But instead of focusing on the promise of Eternal life, this pastor, who I am SURE was well-meaning, bless his heart, focused only on Jesus first words, "Do not let your hearts be troubled."

So he basically looked into the faces of this man's parents who had outlived him, his wife, his two children, and told them not to be troubled. He said that the three grandchildren who would never have memories of him being able to walk or talk or play with them and the one on the way who would have no memory of him at all that they did not need to be troubled. And I sat squirming in my pew and biting my tongue not to yell at him to stop.

But when the minister of their church had her turn, I watched her abandon her written remarks and step away from the pulpit and walk right down to the family and say, "When Jesus offered those words, he did not mean that you should not be troubled ***now***. Anyone who has lost a husband, a father, a grandfather, a son is going to be troubled. It is expected for us to be troubled when we wonder how we will function in the practicality of everyday living without someone so important and vital to our family being by our side. It is expected for us to be troubled when we have watched a cruel disease rob someone we love of his memory and ability to speak and think. It is expected for us to be troubled when we live through the first Father's Day and vacation and Christmas without him here. But Jesus promises us that we can have hope that we will not face this trouble alone. And that he will give you a peace that no one else can give you." I wanted to cheer out loud from my pew that his pastor had rescued the day!

You see, that well-meaning chaplain did not have the right to say that my friends should not let their hearts be troubled. But Jesus does. The moment that the angel of God rolled the tomb away and allowed Jesus to begin his journey back to Galilee,

God had the right to tell us not to be troubled. When the angel tells the women that Jesus will meet them there, Jesus had the right to tell us all not to be afraid. Not to let our hearts be troubled. And the angel of God had the authority to convey the hope, the belief, even the assurance that anyone who believes in the authority of Jesus can give up death. Because Easter is not about human capacities or possibilities or determination. Easter is not about trying just a little harder to get it right or be better or outsmart illness and death. It is about God having the last word and knowing that THAT word is Eternal Life!

If you ever have the privilege of seeing the place where they believe Jesus may have been buried, you will see some of the most beautiful words ever written on the door that has been placed on the low cave. Very simply stated they read, "He is not here, He is risen!" For you and me and everyone who believes in the resurrection of Jesus Christ, that door actually says, "She is not here. They are not here. You are not here." Because all who believe will one day rise as we give up death!

Author Ernest Hemingway is known to have said, "life breaks everyone." And if you have made it to about the 6th grade or beyond, you know this is true. Life is hard. People are not always nice. We do not always get our way. And as a friend of mine often tells her children, "Fair is where pigs are judged!" But because of the life, death and resurrection of God's only son Jesus Christ, life may break us, but death will not! So friends, we can give up death because He is risen. Christ is risen indeed. Thanks be to God! Alleluia! Amen!

The 'I Am' Statements of Jesus

I Am: The Light of the World

Psalm 43:3,4; John 8:12

I am going to ask you to open your minds and unclutter your hearts and lend me your imaginations for a few moments if you will.

My name is Mary of Bethany. I live with my sister Martha and next door to our brother Lazarus and his family. We are all disciples of Jesus of Nazareth. Yes, you heard what I said! As a woman who has never been able to learn directly from a Rabbi, I never thought I would be able to refer to myself as anyone's disciple! Especially Jesus!

You see, we are convinced without a doubt that Jesus is the Messiah that my people, the Jews, have waited on for thousands of years. He is so different from any religious leaders that I know. While many of them seem genuine enough, no priest or member of the Sanhedrin has ever taken a personal interest in Martha and me. But Jesus is different. He knows us so well, knows how different we are from each other and yet, values us both just the way we are.

As soon as I met him, he invited me to sit with Lazarus and the other men in the family to listen to his teachings. He knows that Martha would rather be putting up figs for the winter or sewing our brother's tunics but that I love to listen to his thoughts about God's word. And since disciple simply means "learner" that is what I have become.

I understand that YOU are disciples of Jesus too. That's why I am anxious to tell you about what happened at our annual

Festival of Tabernacles, sometimes called the Feast of Booths. I heard that you don't observe that here in your temple, so let me fill you in on the history.

While we traditionally hold this annual celebration as a time to give thanks to Yahweh for the harvesting of crops, it is also a time to remember how He provided for our ancestors when they journeyed with Moses from Egypt to the Promised Land. Even though the distance was only about 250 miles, as the crow flies, it took them 40 years! But you know how men are about stopping to ask for directions! Miriam, Zipporah and the other women just had to grin and bear it!

Beginning on the eighth day of the seventh month, any Israelites who are able travel to the Temple in Jerusalem. Many build temporary booths around the outskirts of the Temple proper, as a reminder of the blessing that God always provided a place for His people to live, even in the desert. Then everyone dances and sings around the city in remembrance of the Israelites victory over Jericho.

Each morning during the week, priests carry water from the Pool of Siloam and pour it out on the west side of the altar to reminds us that God provided water for our people in the wilderness. And all the people chant from the prophet Isaiah, "With joy you shall draw water from the wells of salvation."

Also, the priests have four HUGE candelabras that are lit in the courtyard of the women. ***They*** are supposed to remind us of the pillar of fire that led the Israelites through the wilderness. The glow from the lights is so bright it can be seen for miles. And the people sing, "Your Word is a lamp unto my feet and a light unto my path!" It truly is breathtaking!

One year, Jesus was staying at Lazarus' house right before the Feast of Booths began and, since Bethany is so close to Jerusalem and we had planned to participate anyway, Jesus went with us. When the water was poured out on the first day, many of us could not help but remember that Jesus had recently said to us, "Let anyone who is thirsty come to me and drink. And I will give you living water." We did not understand what he meant, but it sure did anger some of the Pharisees. They even wanted to arrest him!

Somehow, the Festival didn't seem as much like a celebration as it had in the past. I don't know if my mind was fixed on that living water that Jesus spoke of or if it just seemed out of step with what we were learning from him. And Jesus seemed very different too. As if something was troubling him. Then, as soon as the lamps were lit and the people began to clap and sing, Jesus cried out in a loud, anguished voice, "I AM THE LIGHT OF THE WORLD."

We were stunned. It seemed so out of character for him. It was just not like Jesus to say something that sounded so egotistical. Usually he gives all glory to his heavenly Father. Yet, it was obvious that he was truly grieving. Peter, James and John ran over to him along with Mary Magdalene and put their hands on his shoulders as he leaned over in sorrow.

After a while he composed himself. And all of us, his disciples that is, gathered around him. We knew he had something important to share with us because he sat down. And usually, rabbis just teach while they walk. But Jesus IS different that way. He likes to look into your eyes when he talks about the Father.

He told us that God commanded the people to hold the Festival, said the command is right in the Law of Moses. But all of these other rituals were created by mankind. Then he repeated himself, this time quietly and calmly, "I am the Light of the world. Whoever follows me will never walk in darkness but will have the light of life." Now, I am certainly not a scholar – I was just ALLOWED to start studying the Scriptures, but when he said, "I AM" I think he used the same Hebrew words that God used when he called to Moses out of the burning bush. And my thought must have been right because some of the men gasped when they heard it!

Then Jesus began to speak to us right out of his heart. THIS was the compassionate, approachable Jesus that we love. He said, "There are several things that happened today that grieve me. First, is the manner in which the people have distorted the way they use the Word of God for their own purposes. It is not wicked to pour out water and light candles. But ***"unless the priests and the people lift their minds and hearts to the Lord and experience change, these traditions are futile"***. (1)

Jesus continued, "I want you to understand that the festival itself gives neither light nor life. And unless we are moved by these joys to take them from the Temple and out into the world, they are useless. This light is of man – big manmade candles that shine light that can be extinguished. The light of God will shine forever in our hearts. Those candelabras only represent the good things of the past but don't reflect the love of God that is present today. Or what God hopes you have learned from our past."

Peter of course, spoke for all of us and said, "What were we supposed to learn teacher?" Jesus replied, "God called His chosen people to be a light to the nations. We failed horribly. ***"Israel faces a much greater judgment than the 'unclean' Gentiles because we have been given more light and yet have rejected it."*** (2) The light that they were asked to shine was from God, for God's people. All people! But when they wandered through the desert, they kept it to themselves.

Then Thomas asked, "Is that why YOU are here?" And Jesus smiled for the first time. It seems that is why he said that THOSE WHO FOLLOW HIM will have the light of life. If I understood him correctly, Jesus said that the sun gives light to the world. Physical light. But only God can give light to the soul. Spiritual light. And that when our ancestors just could not catch on to what God intended, God sent us that spiritual light in Jesus. AND that his light is available to all, but only those who follow him will receive it!

I thought it was ironic that the religious leaders, the Pharisees, who are supposed to know everything, were rejecting the light even as it stood among them. They clapped and sang for the candelabras and ignored Jesus while he was in their midst! I think THIS is what upset him so. But I know that God's will always prevails. Because every time I watched a ***crowd*** of people reject Jesus, he simply turned away from them and sought out an individual who needed healing. His love is that personal and his light is that direct.

I think that must be how Jesus wants ***us*** to shine the light. Because Jesus came to be the light of the world, but he calls each of us to receive the light, to walk in it. Personally. So, what I came to believe that day is this: "Jesus is our light and we trust Him; He is our Leader and we follow Him; He is our Life and we grow in Him and reveal Him to this dark world." (Col 1:13-14) We cannot receive the light from history or science or any other discipline unless God's light shines on it first.

And I think Jesus was hurt, and maybe even a little frightened, that there was so much physical light in the Temple but there was still so much darkness in the minds and hearts of those who worshiped there. Didn't they realize that they really had nothing to celebrate as long as they ignored Jesus, the true light, as he shared God's love in so many ways?

And that I why I felt was so important to come here today and talk to you. I can see that you all have the genuine light of Jesus in your eyes and in your hearts. Although this Temple is not like any that I have ever seen before, I am sure it is a wonderful place to be disciples, to learn about God and God's son Jesus. I really feel the power of the Holy Spirit here – especially with your singing.

I am sure you understand that when we fellowship with God and meditate on God's word and obey God's commands that God's light shines "in our hearts to give us the light of the knowledge of God's glory displayed in the face of Christ." (2 Cor 4:6) And I know that today, millions of people profess to be followers of the Lord. What I don't understand is, if that is true, why there is so much darkness. And some days the world seems to get darker and darker.

So, I wanted to tell you how Jesus felt about the worship that took place that day at the Feast of Booths. The church lit festal lights but did nothing to transform the world. I am sure your Temple is not like that. I am sure you all know that – well to use Jesus' own words, "No one lights a light and then puts it under a basket. Instead they put it on a stand so it can give light to everyone in the house!" (Matthew 5:15)

I mean if there is one thing that I learned for certain that day, it's that Scripture won't give you light unless you live by it. So as a fellow disciple, I want to encourage you to shine the light of Jesus in every way you can. Love the loveless and the unlovely and the unlovable. Love yourselves. Love without jealousy or threat or ulterior motives.

Feed those who are hungry and invite them to your worship. Even if they don't look like you or speak your language. Offer hope to those who have none and give help without expecting anything in return. In other words, treat people the way YOU would want to be treated. Like Jesus treats you.

And I truly believe that if we all do these things, the light will shine in the darkness. And the darkness will not overcome it. Amen.

(1) He Walks with Me, Warren Wiersbe, David C. Cook Publishing, Colorado Springs, So, 2016, pg. 50

(2) Ibid, pg. 52

I Am: The Door

John 10:1-10

Two Elders were invited to come to a confirmation class and share their faith experiences. When asked, both men sighted the 23rd Psalm as their favorite. The teacher then asked if each man could recite this beloved passage for the young people. The first man happened to be an English teacher and drama coach. He repeated the Psalm in a powerful way. When he finished, the class clapped enthusiastically and asked him to recite more passages of Scripture.

Instead he deferred to the next gentlemen, who happened to be a contractor. He repeated the same words--'The Lord is my shepherd; I shall not want...' but when he finished, not a sound came from the class. Instead, all of the young people were sitting quietly, awestruck, almost as if they were praying. You literally could have heard a pin drop!

Then the first man stood to his feet. "I have a confession to make," he said. "The difference between what you have just heard from my friend, and what you heard from me is this: I know the Psalm, but my friend knows the Shepherd."

When Jesus told the parable that included the statement "I am the door", he offered it in the context of a much larger scope than we have time to examine today. But it is important for us to know that he tells a crowd of people this story after they have witnessed him healing a blind man. He does this to help some of the people in the crowd understand, namely the Pharisees, that we can have perfect vision but still be spiritually blind. Then he offers this "I Am" statement, which is followed by the reminder that Jesus came so that we could ALL have abundant life.

I tell you this because it makes the words of Jesus so much more powerful. When read all together, these passages remind us that Jesus knows us and calls us by name. God's desire is for everyone to know ***Jesus*** just as well. But only those who recognize his voice and go in and come out through the gate or door that God provides will receive the promise of abundant life. The two stories together remind us that ONLY GOD can decide who to call His own. And that it is God's desire that we all want to live abundantly. So, let's look at this a little more closely.

In ancient Palestine, many different shepherds might bring their flocks into the same village after a day of grazing so the flocks and the shepherds could rest. The sheepfold was where they slept and was usually a circular area, enclosed by rocks that were high enough to keep the sheep from jumping over them. They were topped with briars to keep wolves and other predators from climbing in. Kind of a precursor to barbed wire! The enclosure had one gate and the flocks all mixed in together.

Many might wonder how in the world the shepherds were able to separate the flocks in the morning since all sheep basically look alike. But even though sheep are fairly unintelligent, they know the sound of their shepherd's voice. And they only respond to the voice they know. So each shepherd would stand outside the door, call their sheep by name, and the sheep naturally follow the voice of their own master.

Some theologians will say that this parable is really about the doctrine of election. That God has given a certain number of individuals to Jesus and that, even though Jesus knows how sinful, disobedient and weak we can be, he will call us anyway. But he will only call ***that*** number – the number known ONLY by God. And theologically speaking, this is true. God's has named us and calls us even though we do not deserve it. And God knows who will respond to his call. But I think to the average Joe sitting in the pew, it is more important to think about the tender, personal nature of the shepherd that helps us live abundantly!

In Jesus' day, the shepherd was so intensely interested in every single one of his flock that he could identify them by the sound of their cry and could actually "feel" when one sheep was missing without having to count them. That is the nature of our God who knows us so personally and uses our names to call us.

When I was studying Old Testament at Erskine Seminary, our professor told us the first night of class that his name was William Henry Frazer Kuykendall. One of my fellow classmates asked if we should call him Professor Kuykendall or Dr. Kuykendall, not really knowing what his credentials were. He replied, "The Lord calls me Bill – you can call me whatever you like."

Abundant life means knowing in our hearts that God can call us by our names. But it also means that we must recognize the voice of our shepherd. That's why the confirmation class was so awestruck by the second man who recited Psalm 23. It was clear that he had relationship with God that was deep and wide and high and long.

But there was also another kind of sheepfold that shepherds made use of in Jesus' day. You see, sometimes a shepherd was too far away from a village when night began to fall. In this case he would have to find a makeshift sheepfold, either but corralling the sheep into a cave or by pulling thorny brush around them as walls. Then once the sheep settled down for the night, the shepherd himself would lay down across the entrance and serve as the actual door.

This is the way that we receive the second provision from God for abundant life. Jesus is our door and a door serves two purposes: it keeps things in, and it keeps things out! And knowing that we, like sheep, can also be prone to wander, Jesus is ***our*** door. He offers us safety, but he also gives us the freedom to choose. He even told the people listening that day, "I am the door. Whoever enters by me will be saved and will come in and go out and find pasture." This is because God knows that we need a balance in our lives of time within the sheepfold and time out in the pasture.

When we stay within the sheepfold, we are protected. We are restricted. We are safe. We don't have to make choices – they are made for us. Being in the sheepfold is almost like coming to worship. When you come to church you read what it written, listen to what the pastor chooses or what the choir wants to sing. You don't get to offer feedback or argue with the preacher. You don't really have to make decisions at all. And hopefully your mind is allowed to focus on God and God's word and God's wishes for your life and the life of the church.

This is a description of what Sabbath truly should be about. But not everyone chooses to come into THAT sheepfold.

I have told many a mother who worries about her adult children that no longer find it necessary to attend church on Sunday, that going to church doesn't make you a Christian any more than going to a garage makes you a car. It is God's hope that we will all want to come to church and spend time within the fold being nurtured and surrounded by those who have like values, beliefs and goals. And God will always be calling and waiting in hops that we will enter. But our call as God's sheep would not be complete if we stayed within these walls all the time. A big part of abundant life if taking what you receive within the fold into the world and sharing it.

That is why the shepherd calls the sheep OUT of the sheepfold. We must have the freedom to grow and discover what other options are in the meadow. I read once: "You send a child off to college with simple faith and their she encounters complex doubt." Yet, how can she truly KNOW what she believes if she is never tested, never allowed to explore? Also, it is IN the pasture that we have the opportunity to work and witness for God. It is where we introduce others to God - people who may not have recognized God's voice when God called their name.

Here is another analogy. It is truly a blessing to sit with a group of friends, or church members or family members and talk about the good old days. Our history and our heritage are a huge part of who we are. One of the things I love most about my call to ministry is hearing stories about things that happened at Nazareth in the past.

When I was sitting with Phil and Lane Stone, Ruby Stone's son and daughter-in-law, Phil told me about a summer when he and Steve Collins and Cissy Berry, or Amelia Senn as some of us know her, were in the Youth Group and they went on a mission trip to Mexico and painted a hospital. Ken and Jenny Collins and Harold and Ginny Edge were the chaperones. What a gift of grace that was for him to ***recall*** this time and for me to ***hear*** about it. It was like sitting within the sheepfold.

But God does not call us to glory ***only*** in our past accomplishments. God want us to continue to paint hospitals and feed hungry people and pray with the sick and take the Lord's Supper to those who can no longer come to worship. That is why God calls us OUT of the sheepfold. To share the Good News of salvation through Christ.

Many times, we need walls and fences to keep us in or keep us out. We need food for physical nourishment that is enjoyed in safe and clean places and times of worship that will nourish our souls. We need emotional boundaries to protect ourselves from those who want to hurt us or think only of themselves. But just as we cannot always live in the past, we cannot always stay where it is safe and serene. We must work for God – out in the pasture - in the present kingdom and help build a strong and sturdy sheepfold for future generations.

But there is also a third aspect of this story that I think really speaks to us today. When Jesus first told the parable, many people assumed that the sheepfold was representative of Israel. Of the Jews – God's chosen people. This is understandable. When the Canaanite woman approached Jesus and asked him to heal her daughter who was possessed by evil spirits, Jesus replied, "I was sent only to the lost sheep of Israel."

Yet here in the Gospel of John, Jesus himself seems to realize that God sent him to save the whole world. Perhaps once Jesus was in the world, it reinforced that every child of God is created in God's image and has potential in the kingdom. So, God called the sheep of Israel OUT of the sheepfold and into the world, to minister to the Gentiles.

And Jesus' words, "I am the Door" remind us that abundant life lived to the very fullest involves being in the center of God's will. It's not an easy, sentimental, romantic life. It's one of rugged discipleship. It involves receiving Jesus Christ as your Savior. I could go out and purchase you an elaborately expensive gift and wrap it up and offer it to you. You could very well refuse to accept it.

It is possible to refuse this abundant life which Christ offers. Because something inside each of us knows that answering God's call will reorganize your life. It will cause change. Any kind of change is threatening. You know that. I know that. We human beings, like sheep are creatures of habit. We are resistant to change. There is a strange comfort in the status quo. But each of us has to make a choice — an act of will to receive Jesus Christ as your Savior, acknowledging your need, if you want to experience abundant life.

I'd like to close by reminding you that the Holy Spirit works in mysterious ways! I left the office completely worn out Thursday at 6:30 with no end to this sermon. I slept fitfully, worrying about how to wrap it up along with a lot of other things that I have SOOO much control over like rain and how windy it would be at the grave on Saturday and the mass shooting in New Zealand. I finally decided that sleeping late on my "Sabbath" was not going to work. After breakfast, I pulled up my daily devotion from Henri Nouwen. His words were written about this passage: "I have come that you might have life and have it abundantly. Nouwen wrapped it up for us. Here is what he wrote:

"Our lives are destined to become like the life of Jesus. The whole purpose of Jesus' ministry is to bring us to the house of his Father. Not only did Jesus come to free us from the bonds of sin and death; he also came to lead us into the intimacy of his divine life. He came to lift us up into loving community with the Father. Only when we recognize the radical purpose of Jesus' ministry will we be able to understand the meaning of the spiritual life. Everything that belongs to Jesus is given for us to receive. All that Jesus does we may also do."

Friends, it is my prayer that we will all follow Jesus into the sheepfold for Sabbath and then out into the pasture when called, so that we might fulfill the individual destiny that God has planned for us all. Eternal life in Christ Jesus. Amen.

I Am: The Good Shepherd

John 10:11-18

This morning I am going to ask you to stand and remain standing if you have or have ***ever*** had one of the following characteristics: poor eyesight, stubbornness, or a tendency to overeat. If you find safety in numbers, like to be part of the crowd or consider yourself outgoing, gregarious or social. Please stand if you feel like you are a follower rather than a leader, are frightened easily, do not like loud noises, tend to wander off when you are out with family or friends, cannot relax when you are stressed or grind your teeth when you sleep. Well, those of us who are standing have the same characteristics of sheep! (ask everyone to be seated)

Perhaps that is why Jesus felt it was important to overemphasize our need for a shepherd by spending so much time in the Gospel of John teaching about it. After all, two of the seven "I am" statements found in John's gospel deal with this concept. Last week, we learned that Jesus said "I am the gate" which referred to the opening of the sheepfold or place where sheep sleep. In a continuation of last week's verses, today we hear that Jesus is our Good Shepherd.

The Good Shepherd had long been promised to God's chosen people, the Israelites. The prophet Isaiah says of God: "He will feed his flock like a shepherd; he will gather the lambs in his arms, and carry them in his bosom, and gently lead the mother sheep." (Is 40:11). Ezekiel said, "I will set up over them one shepherd, my servant David, and he shall feed them: he shall feed them and be their shepherd." (Ezekiel 20:24). John's

Revelation contains more than 30 references to God as our shepherd and Jesus as the Lamb of God. Indeed, when John the Baptist saw Jesus, he cried, "Look, the Lamb of God who takes away the sins of the world." (John 1:29).

Those same children of God were often referred to as God's sheep in numerous verses. In the very familiar Psalm 23, in the words that provided our call to worship Psalm 100 and again when Isaiah proclaims: "We all, like sheep, have gone astray" (Is 53:6). I guess that's why almost all of us were standing just a few minutes ago. It is safe to assume that everyone of us here has been lost, will be lost or has the tendency to become lost at one time or another.

When Jesus says, "I am the Good Shepherd, I lay down my life for my sheep" we are given one of the most integral statements of our faith. With this one phrase, we know that Jesus claims us because his Father gave us to him and that he bought us with his own blood. In the Old Testament, sheep were taken as a sacrifice to the Temple to be offered to God. In other words, the sheep died for the shepherd or the one who brought it. Under the new covenant of Jesus, the shepherd dies for the sheep.

And just as God's call to us as sheep is totally an act of grace – that is to say that we have done nothing to deserve it – so is Jesus' insistence to search for us when we are lost. Or perhaps, just when we have ***not yet been found***. My own life story is a case in point.

My parents were both raised in the church but, as young adults and new parents in the 60's, church was just not a priority for them. They did join John Knox Presbyterian when I was about 6 but did not really attend. As a child, Easter to me meant a new dress, purse and white gloves and there are numerous pictures of me in different stages of early childhood modeling my new outfit. This was about the only time I remember going to church. If we prayed or read the Bible, I have no memory of it. I learned the Christmas story from watching "A Charlie Brown Christmas" and can still recite Luke 2 from the King James Version, just a Linus did with his blanket wrapped around his head.

But I distinctly remember the first time I went to children's choir, when I was 8. My mother had heard that the newly hired Director of Music was starting a children's choir and, since I had inherited her love of singing, decided to take me. I can still picture the room, the choir director waving her arms like they were angel's wings. I can still hear some of the songs that we sang. I learned the Nicene Creed when I was 9 because we sang it.

And even at this very moment, I can recall feeling like I had come home when I was in that building. I just knew in my heart that I belonged there. Eventually, after hearing my friends talk about Sunday School, I asked if I could go. My mother would drop me off and come back an hour later. When I asked to stay for church, she came back two hours later. I was literally raised by the church and went by myself until I was about 12.

At that time, someone discovered that my mother also enjoyed music. She was asked to help with the Jr. Hi Choir and said "Yes" and began going to church with me. When the time came, I got active in Youth group, went to "Eva Good" church camp every year from 5th – 10th grade, and "accepted Christ" as my savior at camp when I was 11.

I was 15 when we planned to worship in the newly built sanctuary for the first time. I told my dad that it would mean a lot to me if he and my little brother would come that Sunday but if they didn't, I wouldn't bother them about it again. When we got up Sunday morning, Daddy and my brother were dressed for church. I have said many times that I wish I could remember what John Livingston preached on that day, because my whole family has been active ever since. My dad was ordained as an Elder three years later. He is currently serving his 5th or 6th term, although at a different church. Both my brother and mother are Elders as well and all three have held various leadership positions in the church since that day.

It is clear to me that God sought me out that first night of children's choir. Or even before. I know that He literally called me by name. I just went to sing, but what I received was the birth of a faith that has given me much joy over the years, has sustained me through many trials and made me who I am today. I can say that I have never felt so loved as I do in church but also that the greatest sorrow I ever experienced was when the church let me down. Like all sheep, I have wandered away, doubted, ranted at God, shaken my fist at the sky and wondered where God was.

No matter the circumstances, the Good Shepherd has been there – waiting, watching, guiding, filling me with both peace and unrest. The Shepherd has never left me or given up on me, no matter how far I have wandered. While my family has given up on me and I have even given up on myself, The Good

Shepherd never has. He is always there, with his crook, pulling me back into the fold – sometimes gently and sometimes with painful force.

Why? Why did I feel so at home that night when I was 8? Why have I gone back to the place when I was so filled with love – some might think they had all they need and not return. Why, when the people of the church turned against me, used me as a scapegoat to correct a terrible injustice, did I still turn back to the same fold?

Friends, it is pure grace. The thief has tried to steal me quietly, the robber has tried to abuse me violently, but the Shepherd has never left my side. And the shepherd will never leave your side either. All you have to do is acknowledge that you are God's sheep – totally dependent on the goodness, love and forgiveness of God - even when you cannot see it.

Now if you don't remember anything else that I say this morning, remember this. There is ABSOLUTELY NOTHING SPECIAL ABOUT ME. Other than the beautiful fact that I am created in the image of God. There is NO DIFFERENCE between my story and yours. We are all underserving yet the Good Shepherd laid down his life for each one here. All we must do is believe.

And while we cannot earn this love, this incredible gift, there is a very important verse in this passage that tells us how we can show our gratitude for it. Jesus says: "I have other sheep that do not belong to this fold. I must bring them also, and they will listen to my voice." (v.16) In his book <u>He Walks with Me</u> minister Warren Wiersbe says: "Divine election is not a deterrent to evangelism but one of the dynamics behind evangelism." In other words, we are called to salvation to follow and to serve. We are pulled into the flock so that those who have not joined the fold can find it through OUR stories, through OUR faith experiences, through OUR willingness to share the successes and failures of our lives.

Today, it breaks my heart that so many people try to become the shepherd when it is clearly not our job. God calls us to ***witness*** to the lost, not to save them. And WE do not know who those lost are. But God does. WE do not know other peoples' innermost thoughts, but God does. WE do not know their circumstances or their backgrounds. But God does. WE do not know their hearts. But God does.

You see, only God knows WHO he has yet to bring into the fold and since we do not, we are called to witness to ***everyone***. To ***include*** everyone. To ***accept*** everyone because they TOO are made in the image of God. Jesus alone is the Gate and calls people in and calls people out. He uses our voices, our hands, our arms. But ONLY the Good Shepherd knows who will stay.

My shepherd knows me and understands me thoroughly. He knows what make me tick, what makes me skittish and how far I am willing to witness and to wander. Yet that Shepherd still loves me. You know the person I portray, the thoughts that I share, the stories that I am willing to expose to you and love me if you relate to them or find them helpful in your own life. God knew me before God formed me in my mother's womb and you did not.

So how dare any person, any church, any denomination, indeed any faith presume that we have the knowledge of who has a place in the fold and who does not. As a witness to the lost, we don't know who God's elect are, nor should we worry ourselves about these eternal mysteries. Our commission is to share the Gospel in the power of the Holy Spirit and trust the Lord to call out those who are His.

But friends, here is what we DO know. In the beginning, after God created the Heavens and the Earth and all that was in it, it was too beautiful for God to enjoy alone. And even though he knew we would screw it up, God made humankind in the very image of God so that we could have fellowship with God and each other. God created God's sheep and called us into the sheepfold.

And when it was apparent that we are ALL prone to wander, have poor eyesight, like to overeat, follow the crowd and grit out teeth in our sleep because we cannot control life, God became a human Shepherd that sheep could really see and hear and smell and touch. A shepherd who got tired and sweated and laughed and had sore feet and drank wine at weddings and cried when his friend died. And that shepherd laid down his life. He obediently carried a cross up the hill of salvation. That shepherd bore the pain that my sins and yours caused him and went to Hell and battled the devil for three days so that you and I will never have to. In return, all we have to do is let the Shepherd's crook pull us in the right direction.

Wiersbe again say, "Most of the trouble in our world is caused by people who ignore Christ and insist on having it our own way, and this can and often does happen in our local churches." And friends, those are the sheep that Jesus still hangs on the cross for. You and me. Every day.

You see, the grace of God means that the longer we know Jesus Christ, the more helpless we realize we are. That is called faith. Sometimes we forget. And God reminds us through Scripture, or a song, or a rainbow, or the laugh of a child or the voice of a stranger or in our deepest silence that it is God who made us. And not we ourselves!

When Jesus Christ is our Shepherd, our future is secure. We have nothing to fear. Thanks be to God. Amen.

I am: The Way, the Truth and the Life

John 14:1-14

I don't think I have ever begun a sermon with a disclaimer, so to make up for lost time, I will begin with TWO today. First, my plan during Lent was to preach the seven "I am" sayings one sermon at a time. Seemed logical for the six weeks of Lent, Maundy Thursday and Easter, knowing that I am missing one service. If I had done my homework ahead of time, I would have realized that this "I am" saying, is worthy of THREE sermons – one for the way, one for the truth and one for the life. So, rather than trying to fit eight pounds of nails into a six-pound bag, as my husband likes to say, this morning we will only scratch the surface of the richness of this pastoral conversation from Jesus.

Second, I am well aware of the need to use inclusive language in our modern-day world. I completely empathize with people who have had abusive, neglectful or oppressive past relationships with parents. I TRY to do my best to use language that invites men and women who have a negative connotation of the word "Father" to picture God in the way that suits their needs. HOWEVER, in this conversation, it is clear that Jesus is referring to his Heavenly FATHER in a way that illustrates a loving, caring and nurturing father. In the larger passage that his words are a part of, Jesus uses the word Father 53 times!! So, I will follow Jesus' example in my thoughts today and use "the Father" and the pronoun "he" frequently. Please understand that I do not mean to be hurtful in any way, but rather true to the meaning of Jesus' words.

Somewhere along the way, this verse has become the be-all, end-all verse to hang your hat on to describe ***true*** Christianity. Therefore, it is often overused with a sort of gate-keeping quality – to weed out people who want to have hope that Jesus came to save the WHOLE WORLD! I often wonder what would have happened if past theologians and religious leaders had decided to emphasize, "Sell all you have and give the money to the poor and follow me" instead, but I digress.

However, when we make this "I am" statement into the measuring stick for Christians, we take Jesus' words out of their context. This conversation that Jesus shares with his disciples is part of the longest discourse of Jesus' recorded in all of Scripture. It begins in John 13, when Jesus washes his disciples' feet, and goes through John 17 when Jesus prays for the himself, his disciples, his enemies and then those who have yet to believe. I say this because it is important for us to understand that these words from our savior are completely PASTORAL and not DOCTRINAL. They were given as a comfort and not as a theological truth.

Let's put ourselves in the disciples' sandals for just a moment to understand why they needed to hear this hopeful promise. These twelve men, and most likely their families, have given up everything to follow Jesus of Nazareth. Their livelihood, their safety, their belongings, their past relationships, ALL of the comforts and familiarities of their lives. They have also seen the persecution and even hatred that Jesus has faced by not only the political leaders of the day, but the religious leaders whom many would have thought would allies instead.

And now, Jesus has made it clear to them that he is leaving. Dying! That he will die a terrible death. And that even though he will return for a time, THEY are expected to continue his ministry when he is gone. A ministry that they feel unequipped to carry on and that could also lead to THEIR death. In fact, today we know that every one of the disciples, except John, were ultimately martyred for their faith. And on top of all that, Jesus even told them there is a traitor among them and they don't know who it is!

These beloved friends and followers of Jesus were scared to death. Their leader was leaving them, their futures were uncertain, and they had no idea what to expect when the sun rose each day. So, Jesus is seeking to reassure them, to offer them hope, to uplift their spirits as they set out to share the Gospel in a hostile world.

Now, we can relate to their emotions, even if on a different level. Has anyone here ever felt like God has deserted you? Anyone ever felt overwhelmed by expectations at work, school or within your family? Anyone ever wish there had been some instructions that came with raising children or aging with grace? Anyone ever admired someone who has failed you or lost trust in a friend? Well then, like the disciples, we will be blessed by this "I am" statement because with his words, Jesus is our pastor.

Jesus tells them not to worry because he is going to prepare a place for them and us ***and*** that they know how to get there. Then Thomas puts into words what everyone else is thinking, "How can we know where you are going? We do NOT know the way." And Jesus actually offers answers. Those of us who are human pastors can only offer a listening ear, a hug, a path to help you find God in the midst of your suffering, and a promise to pray for you and with you in the joys and struggles that you face. Jesus offers a way when we are lost, truth when we are ignorant and life when we are spiritually dead.

Yes, friends, when we claim Jesus of Nazareth as our savior and Lord, he is our way. The Greek word might be better translated as "path" or "journey". What Jesus means is that HE knows the way to his Father's house and that he will not only SHOW us the way but provide a path for us to follow and a means of doing so.

Of course, Jesus has already done this with his life. Someone once asked me to help convince their mother to take a very serious step – to choose a path that was far different from the one that she was travelling. I was hesitant and told them, "If I am not careful, I will alienate her". When they asked for clarification, I said, "A wise person once told me that if I shine a flashlight in someone's face, all I will do is anger and blind them. But if I shine the flashlight on the PATH, then they may decide to follow." So rather than giving advice to my friend on what she should do, I simply shined the light on the path that I had taken, praying that it would look attractive to her.

When Jesus said, "I am the way" he meant that he had shown his Father's love so that we could all receive the same blessings by following that way. He shined the light of love on the path that leads to the Father and to Eternal life. God calls those who love him to show His love to others by treating them and ourselves with compassion, fairness, respect and gentleness. By speaking the truth in love and admonishing when needed in ways that build each other up rather than destroys.

Jesus also said, "I am the truth". Of course, he did not mean in the literal sense but in the spiritual sense or on a moral sphere. And where do we find God's truth – why in His word, of course! John actually begins his Gospel by telling us that Jesus is the Word made flesh. That is to say, the LIVING word. Again, we can see God's will for our lives by learning from Jesus. But also, by saturating ourselves in the word of God.

The Apostle Paul lived this better than anyone. He wrote to the Romans: "For whatever was written in former days was written for our instruction, so that by steadfastness and by the encouragement of the scriptures we might have hope." (Romans 15:4) As we believe the word and obey it, God's power works in us and accomplishes God's purposes.

You see, Christianity is not just a doctrine, a creed or a religious system. Christianity is a way of life. That is why Saint Francis once said, "Preach the Gospel every day; use words when necessary." But we cannot demonstrate the truth to others if we do not know what those truths are, nor can we teach it to them.

Fred Craddock tells about then time when he lived in a small town in Georgia where the 30-bed county hospital asked all of the local ministers to take turns being Chaplain for a week. On one of his assigned weeks, a new baby was born. He writes, "I went there about nine in the morning and saw a clan of people gathered, looking through the glass at a little bitty new baby."

"Is it a boy or girl?" "It's a girl." "What's the name?" "Elizabeth." "Is the father here?"

Someone pointed and Fred saw a young man leaning against the wall. "I'm the father," the young man told him. "Baby's name is Elizabeth?" Fred patted his back, "She's a beautiful baby." Elizabeth was squirming--you couldn't hear through the glass--but she was squirming, and red faced. Thinking the father may be concerned, Fred told him, "Now, she's not sick. It's good for babies to scream and do all that. It clears out their lungs and gets their voices going. It's all right." The young man nodded, "Oh I know she's not sick. But she's mad as fire."

Fred said, "Why's she so mad?" "Well wouldn't you be mad? One minute you're with God in heaven and the next minute you're in Georgia." Fred asked, "You believe your daughter was with God before she came here?" "Oh yeah." "You think she'll remember?"

"We'll that's up to her mother and me. We've got to see that she remembers, 'cause if she forgets, she's a goner." This father knew that the Word is the way to Heaven, and it was up to him to share it with this beautiful gift – his new baby daughter.

But we all know it is easy to forget with the pace of life and the noise of the world. Which begs the question: how does one remember? And why is it so easy to forget? Well, one remembers by knowing the truth. And if it we don't, then not only can we NOT share it with others, but we forget it also.

Finally, Jesus said, "I am the life." Of course, we know today that Jesus was talking about Eternal life. Jesus had told the disciples about his death and resurrection, but they could not understand it. And while we may not understand it either we know that it is an historical fact. Jesus of Nazareth was crucified on a cross, suffered on our behalf and died. We know he was buried in a borrowed tomb but when the women went to tend to his body, he was not there. He had risen! As we journey through Lent, seeking to follow Jesus more closely by examining his words and our lives, we can do so with the joy of Easter people, knowing that this promise "I am the life" calls us to live as repentant sinners saved by grace.

Yet, Jesus was not only promising Eternal life but reminding his disciples for all time that we are called to live FRUITFUL lives, as he did. After Jesus' death, resurrection and ascension the disciples planted churches in Jerusalem, Samaria and all throughout the known world. Perhaps in an effort to follow this "I am" statement from Jesus, these churches were called "The Way". And because God's church still lives all over the world today, we know that they were fruitful in their efforts.

Understanding this, the Holy Spirit might be asking us today if NAZARETH is a fruitful church. Luke tells us those first believers in Acts were unified. Are we unified in our beliefs, our mission and our teaching? The first church shared not only their possessions for the good of all, but also their joys and burdens and everyday lives. Do we share what we have so that others can be blessed? They ate and prayed and sang and worshiped and had glad and generous hearts. As a church, we might pause and examine the body of Christ in this place to be sure we are still bearing fruit as Christ's people in the world today.

One thing is certain. We must seek the will of God and ask for the guidance of the Holy Spirit if we are to bear fruit for God. In other words, we can only seek the Father's way, share the Father's truth and hope for life with the Father if we listen to the Spirit. All our discipleship must be human effort that is blessed by the Spirit of God.

Often times, when people give me compliments at the door after worship, you will hear me say something like, "It is all God." Well friends I really believe this. It's not just something they teach us to say because it sounds "preachery". Rev. Bob Cook once said, "If you can explain what's going on, God didn't do it." This describes me and my ministry perfectly. If God can use an ordinary sinner like me to bring His word to one individual, it can only be a combination of human effort and the Holy Spirit. There is no way I can explain it otherwise.

So, by God's grace and out of His great love for each one here, we have received another promise. This promise will journey with us on the Lenten road to Jerusalem and even beyond as we live as resurrection people. Jesus Christ is the way to his Father's house and the truth about his Father's heart. He brought the Father's life to earth so we could share in it now and forever. In the name of the Father and of the Son and of the Holy Spirit. Amen.

I am the Bread of Life

John 6:25-35

Before I read the Scripture, I need to set the scene for us all. There are only two miracles that are reported in all four Gospels. The resurrection of our Lord, Jesus, and the story of Jesus feeding the 5000. Our "I am" statement this morning takes place after the latter, according to John. Jesus and his disciples are near the Sea of Galilee where a large crowd has gathered because of the notoriety that Jesus of Nazareth was gaining. As it got late in the day, one of the disciples realized that there was nowhere nearby to get food.

Even if you have never been to church, you have most likely heard this story. Jesus is given five loaves of bread and two fish and feeds all the people there, with baskets left over. In John's Gospel we are told that, soon after, Jesus senses that some other people are coming to take him by force. He sends his disciples in a boat to the other side of the sea – to Capernaum. He then retreats to the mountains to pray.

It is important for us to know that the people saw all of this happen. They saw the disciples leave without Jesus and saw him go away alone. What they did NOT see was Jesus walking across the water in the night when the disciples were battling a storm. Nor did they see Jesus call Peter out of the boat for a little water-walking with him. All they knew was that, by morning, Jesus was also in Capernaum. Not understanding the logistics but wanting more bread, many of the people who had just been fed got into boats themselves and crossed to the other side to find him. This is where our story picks up. I'll begin reading at verse 25.

READ PASSAGE

Now, many of us may wonder what in the world this has to do with us today. But the truth is that crowds are crowds. Whether they are following Jesus, watching a soccer game, gathered for worship in a church or at a rock concert, there are certain characteristics that will be present in every crowd. A crowd is a group of people united by a common ideology, belief or idea but are usually anonymous to most of the others there. Because a crowd denotes a large number of people, they are usually highly emotional, and their emotions are contagious. Crowds also make us very susceptible to suggestions.

Do you remember last year when I told the story about how the teenagers used to sway in the balcony during the hymns and make me laugh? Well, on graduation Sunday they stood at the front of the church in their caps and gowns and, during the last hymn, started swaying. Soon the choir began to sway with them and before I knew it, the whole church was swaying. This is VERY un-Presbyterian but certainly illustrates crowd mentality!

Well, the same thing happened here, according to John. The people were hungry, and Jesus fed them. I am sure that afterwards, as those who had received the bread told the story over and over, it got a little more fantastic each time. Like any fish tale! The crowd probably went from hungry to nearly on death's door, starving and from being fed with five loaves of bread to manna, falling from Heaven, as in the day of Moses.

Now the crowd has grown, and they are hungrier than ever. But Jesus quickly realizes that the people are hungering for the wrong things. And because all crowds are alike, his lesson applies to us too. Here is what we learn from this "I am" saying.

First of all, the crowd was made up of seekers. And so are we. Isn't that why we are here today? We are seeking, - the Word, fellowship, opportunities for service. However, this crowd was seeking the wrong things. Some were seeking so they would not have to earn their own way. They saw a handout in the works, and they were going to take advantage of it. Follow this guy Jesus and you won't have to fish or harvest or hunt. He just gives out lunch!

Some were seeking because of the sensationalism that Jesus' actions were causing. Healing the sick, restoring sight to the blind, demons being sent into herds of pigs. Honestly, it is just human nature to be curious. I often wonder as I wait my turn in the grocery line, how those tabloids can write what they do and not get sued? After all, if they ***are*** true, Jennifer Aniston is constantly pregnant, the princesses in England are mortal enemies and no marriage in Hollywood lasts more than 37 days! But just by the fact that I have READ all these headlines while waiting, we have to assume people actually buy the magazines!

But when Jesus doesn't immediately feed them, they start to question him. To wonder who he really is. They even ask for a sign to prove that he is a miracle worker. After all, THEY WANT THEIR BREAD! The contagion of the crowd is soon sighting Moses and the children of Israel and asking for him to feed them day and night, as Moses did.

Jesus recognizes their misconception and tells the people there, "It was not Moses who gave them food but my Father in Heaven." And this is when we learn the first lesson. The crowd gathered there was seeking the wrong things. They were focused on the human, physical needs but not their spiritual needs. They were thinking only of themselves and not of others and certainly NOT God. And aren't we ALL guilty of asking for things we don't really need?

Jesus tells the all that the bread they seek is perishable. It will only last for a while. But that he can give them something that will last forever. Instead of asking what he means, they offer to work a little first if they will feed him. What must we DO to earn our bread? How can we please God so God will feed us?

The people are seeking the wrong thing. They are seeking what will satisfy their immediate need and not what will fulfill them on a long-term basis. In our world of free shipping, Amazon Prime, Venmo me what you owe me and just put it in the microwave, we too often seek what we want WHEN we want it, rather than waiting for God's timing on something that could be better. We seek the immediate rather than the eternal.

We also see that the people are seeking in the wrong way. As I said, the people offer to work a little for the bread, if that is what it takes. This show us that they want to give their time but not themselves, their hearts. Jesus points out that they cannot work for the things that God will give them – God gives to us out of God's grace and love. All they have to do is bring believing hearts to God and God will fill them to the brim! But before we judge the crowd too harshly, has anyone here ever tried to bargain with God for what we think we need? We, too, can seek in a way that shows that we trust more in ourselves than in God's plan for our lives.

One of my favorite quotes is an Arabian proverb that says, "If God answered the prayers of dogs, it would rain bones". Faith calls us to believe that God provides for us in just the right way at just the right time. That way, when we ask for things that are not for our good and God's glory, we do not receive them. That is why we ask each week in the Lord's Prayer: give us this day our ***daily*** bread. Jesus didn't tell us to pray for a whole month's worth! If we trust not only in God but in God's timing, we can be assured that God will take care of us.

Jesus then says, "I am the bread of life." Jesus told them that if they accepted THIS kind of bread, they would never be hungry or thirsty. He tells them that the Father gives him everything that he needs so that he can share it with us. That once a child of God gives Jesus their whole heart, that God will never let go of them. What a promise! But the crowd did not understand what this meant, as we do today, and still wanted to just fill their bellies.

Finally, John tells us that, while all of the crowd came seeking something from Jesus, some were seeking half-heartedly. If we had the time to read the rest of John 6, we would learn that many of the followers, when they heard him offer the bread of life, understood and gave God their hearts. But just as many left, grumbling. The wanted ***what*** they wanted, ***when*** they wanted and were not willing to change their expectations. They went away hungry.

This is also something we have in common with the crowd that day. The truth is that sometimes we do not know what we need. Therefore, we cannot recognize it when it is right in front of us. There is a story of a man who owned an icehouse. One day he lost his watch – the one his grandfather had given him- in the sawdust. Saddened, he offered a large reward to anyone who could find it. His workers went through the sawdust, raking, getting splinters in their fingers, hoping for the reward. But no one was successful, and they all went home.

A few minutes after the workers gave up, a small boy came into his office with the watch in hand. The man was overjoyed and wanted to know how he found it when no one else could. The boy explained, "I just lay down in the sawdust and listened. Finally, when I was quiet enough, I heard the watch ticking."

Friends, Jesus offered us this "I am" saying so that we could all understand that God wants us to seek him where he can be found. In Jesus Christ. That God want us to seek him for ourselves, out of our recognition that we need God in our lives. And that God wants us to seek him with our whole heart.

In his Sermon on the Mount, Jesus said: "Blessed are those who hunger and thirst for righteousness, for they will be filled". The kind of hunger and thirst that we have known in our lives, that the crowd knew that day, can hardly be called by that name. Most of us say we are starving when we don't want to take the time to cook and order a pizza instead. God calls us to hunger and thirst for things that will fill our hearts and minds and souls.

And that is why Jesus makes this wonderful offer. He says, "I am the bread of life. When you seek the bread of life and accept it from me, you will never hunger and thirst again". Eugene Peterson explains it this way in The Message: "I came down from heaven not to follow my own whim but to accomplish the will of the One who sent me. This, in a nutshell, is that will: that everything handed over to me by the Father be completed—not a single detail missed—and at the wrap-up of time I have everything, and everyone put together, upright and whole. This is what my Father wants: that anyone who sees the Son and trusts who he is and what he does and then aligns with him will enter *real* life, *eternal* life. My part is to put them on their feet alive and whole at the completion of time."

As we come to the Table today, we are reminded that this promise is for all time. There is something important that I have not pointed out explicitly enough about all of the "I am" sayings but that I feel is relevant today. When Jesus tells us "I am", he uses the very same word that God gave Moses when he called him to lead the people out of slavery in Egypt. Moses asked God, "Who shall I say sent me?" God said, "Tell them the God of your ancestors sent me" Moses then said but what if they want to know your name? What shall I say to them?

God replied, "Tell them I am who I am." The Hebrew word is Yahweh. But the word is more fully translated this way: "I am who I am, and I was who I was and I will be who I will be." This is the word that Jesus used in each of his "I am" statements. This is who meets us at the Table today. The bread of life who was and is and always will be is what we remember today. Ever [illegible] Father and of the Son and [illegible]

I Am: The Vine

John 15:1-8

Maundy Thursday is the day that commemorates Jesus' last meal with his disciples. On that night Jesus instituted the Lord's Supper and afterwards, washed the disciples' feet. When all of this had been accomplished, he asked his closest friends, "Do you understand what I have done for you?" Jesus wanted them to be clear of his motives because he knew that soon, he would be facing execution.

Jesus then answered his own question by pointing out that he had taken the form of a servant in washing their feet. Then he commanded them to go and do likewise. Jesus wanted to remind us ALL of who WE are in the grand scheme of things, framed in this act of self-giving love. The Thursday before Easter has thus become known as Maundy Thursday because the word "Maundy" is a shortened form of "mandatum", the Latin word for "command". Jesus' last command before his crucifixion was that we would love and serve one another.

But since we have been working our way this Lenten season through all of the "I am" statements that Jesus gave us in the Gospel of John, I had designated tonight to be the night we immerse ourselves into the words, "I am the vine." Imagine my delight when my studies revealed that the word "prune" used in the parable we just heard is also translated as "cleanse". And that very word comes from the same root of the Greek word that John used when he told us that Jesus washed his friends' feet. Therefore, to cleanse and to prune carry the same meaning in these two stories. Both are God's way of preparing us to share God's holiness and love one another.

It is also important to know that this is one of TWO "I am" statements that was given in the company of his disciples only, along with "I am the way, the truth and the life". One statement was given privately to Martha. You will hear about that one on Easter morning. The others were all given to the crowds that were listening. Therefore, the words "I am the vine, you are the branches" are given very intentionally to Jesus' disciples. You and me!

What instruction does Jesus give us when he tells us this parable? The characters in the allegory are easy to identify. The vine grower is God. It is God who made us. Each of us is from the work, the grace and the imagination of the one true God. Just as no one here can manufacture fruit, no one here can create another living, breathing being. That is left to God and God alone.

Jesus of course is the vine. Many people picture a vine as something that is running or creeping but actually, in the context of grapes, the vine is the thick stalk that connects the branches that are laden with fruit to the roots. Thus, Jesus is the only way that we are connected to the grower, the Maker. The vine sends nutrients from the soil to the branches, which of course is us. Finally, this leads to fruitful branches – our discipleship.

But Jesus is more specific because he says that he is the TRUE vine. This means that Jesus is the original – there are no other copies. Therefore, the ONLY way we can be connected to God is through Christ. To believe in Jesus as our Savior and to be in communion with him. And we know that cannot have communion with God unless we are in UNION with Jesus. Trusting, obeying and living in commitment to him.

So, as we come to the table and remember the night that Jesus shared the Holy Meal with his closest friends and then washed their feet as a sign of loving service, how does this prepare our hearts, our minds and our discipleship to follow his command? Well first, we are reminded that, as the vine grower, God often has to prune us, to cleanse us, in order for us to bear fruit. And just as a farmer may prune seemingly healthy branches for a better end result, even good things sometimes must be cut off from our lives in order for our ministry to be more productive.

Abraham had to leave his home, to be cut off from his people, in order to be the Father of God's nation. David had to leave the simple life of shepherding and writing songs to become a warrior and a King for God and God's people. Joseph had to stand up publicly for Mary, knowing that many people would be unbelieving and turn against him. The Apostle Paul had to relinquish his status of being a member of the prestigious Pharisees in order to build a church for the Gentiles. All of these are examples of God pruning those whom God had called to service.

Many of you have heard me allude to a time of personal difficulty that I experienced in my home church – the only church I had ever known, that I had attended by myself as a child. It was THE place in the world where I always felt loved and cherished and looked up to. But at one point in my life, when I spoke the truth in love, I was not accepted by those who did not want to hear the truth. And so, for a time, I had to leave that church.

As I healed from the experience, I recognized that God was pruning me. You see, I was so comfortable in this one place. I thought the body of Christ lived there and there alone. The result was that I had unknowingly begun to worship my church more than I did my God. So, God took that church away from me.

But during this time of pruning, I grew closer to God. I understood that God alone had to be the foundation of my faith – not a building or a group of people. Finally, I accepted that God meant for the ministry I was being led to, to go beyond the walls of one particular building. It was that pruning that led to my ordination to ministry and finally, to accepting the call to be your pastor.

And just as God as the vine grower knows exactly what we need, when we need it, we cannot receive it if we do not abide in Christ. To make this point clear, Jesus uses the word "abide" ten times in seven verses. Abide is actually defined as "an inward enduring of a personal communion". It means being closer to God through our understanding of who Jesus is and what he has done for us in his life, death and resurrection.

Do any of you remember the old Russian nesting dolls? They are a set of wooden figures which separates, top from bottom, to reveal a smaller figure of the same sort inside, which has, in turn, another figure inside of it, and so on. This is the picture that comes to my mind when I read Jesus' words. God is the big doll and inside is Jesus and the subsequent dolls are each of us, nesting close to the Father and the Son, Abiding in Christ.

But greater communion is not guaranteed unless each of us works hard to develop and maintain our relationship with Jesus as our savior. While God gives us everything we need, through the grace of Jesus and the presence of the Holy Spirit, we must do our part through prayer, reading of Scripture, relationship with others in the body of Christ and obedience to the work that God calls us to.

In *The Message*, Eugene Peterson writes it this way: "Live in me. Make your home in me just as I do in you. In the same way that a branch can't bear grapes by itself but only by being joined to the vine, you can't bear fruit unless you are joined with me". So, we are to be at home in Christ. And the way that Jesus describes this abiding life is what links this "I am" statement to his words after he washed the disciples' feet. But these words are not just for us individually. They are also for us collectively, as the body of Christ on earth.

The love command that Jesus gives in the upper room with the disciples is THE imperative moment in Jesus Christ's teachings that prevents each of us and all of us, as the church, from being inward turned and self-contained. We are to cling to God through Christ in order to bear the fruits of love to each other and for each other. And we are to be obedient to Jesus' command.

Max Lucado gives a perfect illustration in the book that a couple of our Sunday School classes have been studying, Anxious for Nothing. He writes, "When a father leads his four-year-old son down a crowded street, he takes him by the hand and says, 'Hold on to me.' He doesn't say, 'Memorize the map' or 'Take your chances dodging the traffic' or 'Let's see if you can find your way home.' The good father gives the child one responsibility: 'Hold on to my hand'."

This is what Jesus means when he says, "I am the vine – abide in me." In other words, God gives us EXACTLY what we need to love and serve others. But there is also an important message for us collectively. Because I believe that we are being told to abide in each other as well. We are to be the branches that bear one another up. Let me explain.

When I was growing up, my granddaddy had a grape arbor on his farm. Sometimes when we went to visit, some of the grapes would be hanging low to the ground. I loved this because it meant that I could just reach out and pull a few off and eat them, right on the spot!

But sometimes all the grapes would be up high, like Granddaddy had wound them all around the top just so I couldn't get to them. What I didn't know was that he had been "tucking" the branches before the grapes began to form. That is, to control pests and make harvesting easier, he would take low hanging branches and wind them up around branches that were closer to the guide wires. Tucking means branches that may be weaker or more vulnerable are woven in and through stronger, more stable ones. This actually protected the grapes and made them healthier and fuller.

And isn't that what we are called to do in the church? When our brother or sister is hanging low – experiencing a faith crisis, wading through financial difficulties, working hard on a marriage that is failing or dealing with illness or grief – we are to tuck the low-hanging branch closer to the sturdy ones.

The Apostle Paul tells the Romans that those of us who are strong and able in the faith need to step in and lend a hand to those who falter. (Romans 15:1) And that is exactly what Jesus tells his disciples before he goes to his death. I have fed you. I have cleansed you. I have become your servant because I love you and together, we can bring glory to God. Now, when I am gone, do this for the rest of the world.

So as we come forward and remember that meal that has become the most sacred feast of our faith, may we remember that it is God alone who made us; that in order to be fruitful servants we are to make it our aim to cling to Christ'; and that we are commanded by Jesus to serve others with the love that we have been served with. In this way, we will bear fruit for God, glorifying God as we make disciples for Christ. In the name of the Father and of the Son and of the Holy Spirit. Amen.

I am: The Resurrection and the Life

Luke 24:1-12; John 11:1-6, 17-27, 38-44

For those of you who have not been with us throughout the Lenten season, I have been preaching a sermon series on Jesus' "I am" statements from the Gospel of John. Four of his messages were given to everyone who had gathered there. Jesus proclaimed to those following him out of loyalty or curiosity, "I am the Light of the world, I am the Gate, I am the Good Shepherd and I am the Bread of Life". To his disciples only, Jesus revealed, "I am the Way, the Truth and the Life and I am the Vine."

On the first Sunday of Lent, we had a visit from Lazarus' sister Mary. And as John records it, only ONE statement was given privately. "I am the Resurrection and the Life". His words to Lazarus OTHER sister Martha. So, it seems only fitting that we should hear Martha's thoughts on this Easter Sunday. Therefore, I am going to ask you to open your hearts and unclutter your minds and lend me your imaginations for a few moments, if you will.

My name is Martha. I have lived in the town Bethany, a little east of Jerusalem my whole life, with my sister Mary and my brother Lazarus. We are blessed in many ways. Our parents left us very well off and we are also well respected in our little town. Because of this we have tried to give back to our community in whatever ways we can and to be champions of faith in the one true God, the God of Abraham, Isaac and Jacob.

I LOVE to entertain. I am never happier than when I have an excuse to organize and cook and clean. I am ALWAYS busy – it seems to keep me out of trouble. So, we have lots of dinner parties and almost every Shabbat, some of our friends from the Temple come to share the Sabbath meal with us. Honestly, I am never more in my element than when we have guests.

My sister is more of a quiet friend, one who will deliver the meal after I prepare it and then sit and pray with you. She sits with Lazarus so often while he reads the Scriptures that he has even taught HER to read, something most unusual for women in our day. She says she like to read the Psalms and the prophets to friends who are looking for consolation or hope. How two sisters could be so different is beyond me but, in the end, I guess we make a good team.

But Lazarus of course, is the real head of the household and very respected by the Rabbis and other leaders of the Temple. However, he caused quite a stir with some of the Pharisees when our little family became followers of Jesus, the one we ***now know*** is the Christ. Some still say he is only a prophet, but our family believes he is the Messiah, the Son of God, the promised one of the Scriptures who has come to save us all from our sins.

Now that you know a little about us, I want to tell you what happened just a few weeks before Jesus' death. One day Lazarus came in from Temple and clearly had a fever. He was coughing and perspiring and struggling to breathe. We called for the village healer who prepared some tonics for my brother, but he only grew worse. Mary sat by his bedside for many nights, soothing his forehead with a cool cloth and reading the words of King David to him while I prepared soups and broths and herbal teas, one after another. But nothing seemed to help him.

Finally, I couldn't stand it anymore and I told Mary, "We have to DO something!" Her idea of reading Scripture was a good one – I am sure it kept him calm. But let's be practical! This was a time for action. Lazarus always says that if I wrote a Proverb it would be: "Don't just sit there, DO SOMETHING!" But Mary's would be, "Don't just do something, sit here!"

And for once we agreed and Mary had a wonderful idea. She suggested we send word to Jesus, whom we had seen perform healing miracles, to come and lay hands on our brother. Surely, if anyone could heal Lazarus, it was the Great Physician! We found a messenger who ran to give Jesus the news. Lazarus and Peter are Jesus' closest friends and we knew he would come right away. So we were saddened beyond belief and very disillusioned when Jesus went to Judea instead. And to make a long, sad story short, our brother died.

Mary and I could not believe it! Our whole world changed in just a matter of days. What would we do without Lazarus, our beloved brother and head of our household? While we are modern women in a sense, Lazarus was still the real decision maker and took care of all of our business needs. And we love him so! We felt as if no amount of time would heal our hearts.

Then we heard through the village grapevine that Jesus was coming after all. Mary, being Mary, said we should just wait and see what happened. That Jesus would come to us in his time.

Her faith always seems so much stronger than mine. But of course, I didn't listen to a word she said.

I immediately ran to the edge of the village before he could even get to our house. I planned to be diplomatic for once, but that is so unlike me. Instead, as soon as I saw him, I just blurted out, "If you had been here, our brother would not have died." What a bold thing to say to our Lord. In fact, my words and my thoughts really surprised me. We had so much faith in Jesus. But my actions let me know that, even though I did not DISTRUST the Lord, I really didn't really trust him completely. Maybe you can relate.

In truth, while Mary just sits quietly in prayer, I know she has heard me cry aloud more than once, "Why?" or "How?". And this time my only thought was "WHAT IF?" Maybe you have asked the same questions. Looking back now I realize that I have a faith that sometimes limits God – limits his work to the time and place that suits me. Because I followed by saying, no, really begging Jesus, "Even now I know that God will give you what you ask!" You see, I had faith, as long as it followed my plan for action!

Jesus did not seem offended or upset. He was so calm. He placed his hand on me gently and said, "Martha, your brother will rise again". Well as much of a miracle worker as Jesus is, it seemed he didn't understand what I meant. I wanted action and I wanted it then! But in an effort ***not*** to sound irreverent I DID say, "I know that! If there is one thing you have taught us to believe it is that we all will rise on the day of resurrection."

Can you imagine that I talked to the LORD that way? Looking back, it is a wonder that I am still here! But Jesus is always gracious, slow to anger and steadfast in love. Honestly, I have never seen anyone whose eyes were more filled with love as in that very moment. Then he steadied me and said with both gentleness and force. "I am the resurrection and the life. Those who believe in me, even though they die, will live. And everyone who lives and believe in me will never die." Then he said so gently, "Do YOU believe this?"

And friends, I DID! In that moment, I understood something that I had not before. Maybe, it was the wisdom that Mary gleaned from sitting so quietly at the Master's feet. But the whole realm of Jesus' teachings seemed to enter my heart and fill me with peace.

Jesus was telling me that resurrection begins the very moment we believe that he is the Messiah. I realized that, with his words, Jesus had moved resurrection from being just an idea or a concept or even a belief to an actual person. HIM. Jesus of Nazareth. That everything about THIS life takes on new meaning when we are certain of the next life. Of being with those I love who have already died at that very moment – Lazarus and our parents, friends, aunts and uncles. That all of them are just waiting for me and yet with me now!

I will tell you that I don't know how it happened, but I knew there was something holy, something otherworldly that mysteriously connected us all. And even though my heart still ached because of my grief, I had no fear about the future anymore. I knew without a doubt that I would see Lazarus again, in God's time, and that would be just fine. Jesus' promise filled me with hope – not just for the future – but for the present. Somehow, I knew that Jesus had given me the faith to believe in the power of resurrection. And I received that power right then.

And Jesus could see that my heart had changed. So, he asked me to take him to my sister and I did. I wanted to tell her everything but for once, I was as calm and quiet as she was. I think I knew in my heart that Mary needed to have a personal encounter with Jesus in order to receive peace, just as I had.

I led Jesus, and our friends followed, and when we arrived, we found Mary weeping. Have you heard that when Jesus saw her, he began to weep too? Friends, I know he was truly sad that Lazarus was dead, but I believe he was weeping because WE were weeping. Maybe this will give you comfort when you sit in sadness and feel so alone because your loved one is not here with you. When you face anger because your husband has gone and left you with a mess or confusion because you didn't expect to lose a child before you lose yourself, then perhaps the picture of Jesus sitting right beside you weeping WITH YOU, as he wept WITH Mary will be of help. Maybe that deep love and compassion will be what gets you through until morning's light.

After Jesus talked to Mary, the three of us went to the grave where Lazarus had been dead for FOUR DAYS. By this time, the word had spread about what was going on and many people were following us – friends and strangers. And when Jesus called for our dead brother to come out of the tomb, I just blurted out, "But Jesus he will smell so awful!"

Mary gave me the "couldn't you show a little sensitivity and diplomacy for once" look that I have often received, though even SHE seemed confused. Especially when Jesus followed with a prayer "Thank you Father for always hearing me", even before anything happened. Everyone around was so perplexed but I knew in my heart that a miracle was unfolding right before our eyes. And sure enough, Lazarus walked out, shook off his graveclothes and we all went home to celebrate in Martha style. Of course, our joy was short lived because only a few days later, Jesus was crucified. He suffered so horribly and was not even given a proper burial. And that is why Mary and I went with the other women to his tomb, to anoint the body of our beloved savior.

I know that the very reason you are here today is because just as Jesus did not leave Lazarus in the tomb, God did not leave his Son there either. The stone had been rolled away from the entrance to the tomb and two angels told us not to waste time looking for Jesus because he was alive! And he was!

And as Mary Magdalene and Peter ran to tell the others, I remembered the precious moment I had with Jesus. When his words changed my whole life. "I AM THE RESURRECTION AND THE LIFE. THOSE WHO BEILEVE IN ME EVEN THOUGH THEY DIE WILL LIVE AND EVERYONE WHO LIVES AND BELIEVES IN ME WILL NEVER DIE!"

And here is what I have come to know, even in my very busy heart. God's love does not prevent us from experiencing pain or suffering. Yet "The Lord can move into 'dead' and seemingly hopeless situations, and by his resurrection power, transform people and circumstances and infuse life that make everything new." (1)

You know, when Jesus raised Lazarus from his tomb, what he really said was, "Unbind him and let him go!" And oh, what a hope we all have. Because one day, we too will be unbound and let go and will live in His eternity with Jesus! In the name of the Father and of the Son and of the Holy Spirit. Amen.

(1) He Walks with You, David C. Cook, Colorado Springs, 2016. Pg. 98.

CPSIA information can be obtained
at www.ICGtesting.com
Printed in the USA
JSHW011250141219
2899JS00002B/2